THE PURITY TEXTS

Companion to the Qumran Scrolls, 5

Other volumes in the Companion to the Qumran Scrolls series:

The Damascus Text by Charlotte Hempel
The Temple Scroll and Related Texts by Sidnie White Crawford
Pesharim by Timothy H. Lim
The Exegetical Texts by Jonathan G. Campbell
The War Texts by Jean Duhaime

THE PURITY TEXTS

Hannah K. Harrington

T & T CLARK INTERNATIONAL
A Continuum imprint
LONDON • NEW YORK

To my loving husband and dearest friend,
Bill Harrington

Published by T&T Clark International
A Continuum imprint
The Tower Building, 11 York Road, London SE1 7NX
15 East 26th Street, Suite 1703, New York, NY 10010

www.tandtclark.com

British Library Cataloguing-in-Publication Data
A catalogue record for this book is available from the British Library.

Typeset by Data Standards Ltd, Frome, Somerset BA11 1RE
Printed in Great Britain by CPI Bath

ISBN 9780567045294

Contents

Acknowledgments

This work would not have been possible without the invaluable support of several people. I want to thank Professor Joseph Baumgarten, who is clearly the expert on the subject of Jewish purity in Second Temple and Rabbinic times, for the time and energy he has spent in reading copies of this manuscript. He has always been available to consider my questions, and without his input this work would not have come to fruition. Nevertheless, the responsibility for all errors is entirely my own.

My first interest in the subject of purity in ancient Judaism came from my tutelage under Professor Jacob Milgrom as a graduate student at the University of California, Berkeley. Essentially, this work is an update of my research on the Dead Sea Scrolls, published in my doctoral dissertation *The Impurity Systems of Qumran and the Rabbis* (Scholars Press, 1993). In the last decade, many new fragments have come to light which contain data on purity and these have now been collected in this volume, organized and analysed systematically. I continue to gain new insights from the definitive and exhaustive research Professor Milgrom has contributed to scholarship on impurity in the Bible and the ancient world. Also, from the University of California, another mentor, Professor Daniel Boyarin continues to sharpen my understanding of early Judaism and has graciously read and provided advice on parts of this work.

Sincere thanks also go to Philip Davies, for help in preparing the manuscript and organizing it into a serviceable handbook. I appreciate the conversations which forced me to evaluate my ideas and often consider new ones.

My colleague and friend Dr Rebecca Skaggs, together with her late sister Dr Priscilla Benham and late mother Dr Bebe Patten, have always been a source of inspiration for my academic endeavours and for that I am grateful. I particularly appreciate Rebecca for patiently listening to me fuss over difficulties in interpreting obscure texts. I thank my family for enduring the times when I was too busy studying a passage or looking up citations to give them the time they unquestionably deserved. My husband, Bill Harrington, especially deserves a medal for his listening ear, helpful suggestions and loving support.

Abbreviations

Ag. Ap.	*Against Apion*
Ant.	*Antiquities*
DJD	Discoveries in the Judaean Desert
DSD	*Dead Sea Discoveries*
par.	*parashah*
HTR	*Harvard Theological Review*
JBL	*Journal of Biblical Literature*
JJS	*Journal of Jewish Studies*
JQR	*Jewish Quarterly Review*
JStJud	*Journal for the Study of Judaism*
JSOT	*Journal for the Study of the Old Testament*
Jub.	*Jubilees*
Jdt.	Judith
Macc.	Maccabees
PEQ	*Palestine Exploration Quarterly*
RevQ	*Revue de Qumrân*
SAOC	Studies in Ancient Oriental Civilization
SBL	Society of Biblical Literature
Scot J Th	*Scottish Journal of Theology*
Sib. Or.	Sibylline Oracles
STDJ	Studies on the Texts of the Desert of Judah
T. Levi	Testament of Levi
Tob.	Tobit

Biblical Books

Chron.	Chronicles
Deut.	Deuteronomy
Exod.	Exodus
Ezek.	Ezekiel
Gen.	Genesis
Heb.	Hebrews
Isa.	Isaiah

Jer.	Jeremiah
Joel.	Joel
Jn	John
Josh.	Joshua
Kgs	Kings
Lev.	Leviticus
Lk.	Luke
Mk	Mark
Mt.	Matthew
Neh.	Nehemiah
Num.	Numbers
Ps.	Psalms
Pss. of Sol.	Psalms of Solomon
Sam.	Samuel
Zech.	Zechariah

Tractates of the Mishnah (m.), Tosefta (t.) , Babylonian (b.) and Jerusalem (y.) Talmuds

Ar.	*'Arakin*
AZ	*'Abodah Zarah*
BB	*Baba Batra*
Ber.	*Berakhot*
Git.	*Gittin*
H̱ag.	*H̱agigah*
H̱ul.	*H̱ullin*
K̄el.	*K̄elim*
Ma'as. Sh.	*Ma'aser Sheni*
Makh.	*Makhshirin*
Meg.	*Megillat Ta'anit*
Men.	*Menaḥot*
Miq.	*Miqva'ot*
MQ	*Mo'ed Qatan*
Naz.	*Nazir*
Neg.	*Nega'im*
Nid.	*Niddah*
Oh.	*Ohalot*
Par.	*Parah*
Pes.	*Pesaḥim*
Qid.	*Qiddushin*
Rsh	*Rosh ha-Shanah*

San.	*Sanhedrin*
Shab.	*Shabbat*
Sot.	*Sotah*
Tam.	*Tamid*
Ter.	*Terumot*
Toh.	*Tohorot*
TY	*Tebul Yom*
Yad.	*Yadayim*
Yeb.	*Yebamot*
Zab.	*Zabim*
Zeb.	*Zebaḥim*

Related Rabbinic Literature

ARN A	*'Abot de-Rabbi Natan, version A*
Gen. R.	*Genesis Rabba*
Lev. R.	*Leviticus Rabba*
Num. R.	*Numbers Rabba*
PRK	*Pirke de-Rab Kahana*
Sif. meṣ. zab.	*Sifra meṣoraʿ zabim*
Sif. shem. sher.	*Sifra shemini sheraṣim*
Sif. taz. neg.	*Sifra tazri'a nega'im*
Sif. Num.	*Sifre Numbers*
Targ. Ps.-Jon.	*Targum Pseudo-Jonathan*

Editions, Translations, Bibliographies

Editions

Baillet, M.

1962 *Les 'petites grottes' de Qumran Grotte* (DJD, III; Oxford: Clarendon Press).

1982 *Qumrân Grotte 4.[3]III (4Q482–4Q520)* (DJD, VII; Oxford: Clarendon Press).

Baumgarten, J.

1996 *Qumran Cave 4, XIII: The Damascus Document (4Q266–273)* (DJD, XVIII; Oxford: Clarendon Press).

1999b *Qumran Cave 4 XXV: Halakhic Texts* (DJD XXXV; Oxford: Clarendon Press).

García Martínez, F. and E. Tigchelaar

1998 *The Dead Sea Scrolls Study Edition.* Vols. I-II. (Leiden: E.J. Brill).

Milgrom, J.

1994a 'The Purification Rule', in *The Dead Sea Scrolls: Hebrew, Aramaic, and Greek Texts with English Translations. Vol. I: Rule of the Community and Related Documents*, ed. J.H. Charlesworth (Tübingen: J.C.B. Mohr [Paul Siebeck]; Louisville, KY: Westminster/John Knox Press): 177–79.

Qimron, E. and J. Strugnell

1994 *Qumran Cave 4 V: Miqṣat Ma'aśe ha-Torah* (DJD, X; Oxford: Clarendon Press).

Schiffman, L.

1994a 'Ordinances and Rules' and 'Sectarian Rule 5Q13', in *The Dead Sea Scrolls: Hebrew, Aramaic, and Greek Texts with English Translations. Vol. 1: Rule of the Community and Related Documents*, ed. J.H. Charlesworth (Tübingen: J.C.B. Mohr; Louisville, KY: Westminster/John Knox Press): 132–75.

Tov, E. with the collaboration of S. J. Pfann

1993 *The Dead Sea Scrolls on Microfiche: A Comprehensive Facsimile Edition of the Texts from the Judaean Desert* (Leiden: E.J. Brill).

Wise, M.

1991 *A Critical Study of the Temple Scroll from Qumran Cave 11* (SAOC, 49; Chicago, IL: University of Chicago Press).

Yadin, Y.

1977 *Megillat ha-Miqdash (The Temple Scroll).* Vols. I-III (Jerusalem: Israel Exploration Society) (Hebrew).

1983 *The Temple Scroll.* Vols. I-III. (Jerusalem: Israel Exploration Society).

Preliminary Editions and Descriptions of Cave 4 Fragments

Baumgarten, J.

1992a 'The Disqualifications of Priests in 4Q Fragments of the "Damascus Document", a Specimen of the Recovery of Pre-Rabbinic Halakha', in *The Madrid Qumran Congress:*, II; ST DJ 11; (eds. J.T. Barrera and L.V. Montaner Leiden: E.J. Brill); 503–13.

1992b 'The Purification Rituals of DJD 7', *The Dead Sea Scrolls: Forty Years of Research*, eds. D. Dimant and U. Rappaport (Leiden: E.J. Brill): 199–209.

1994a 'Liquids and Susceptibility to Defilement in New 4Q Texts', in *The Community of the Renewed Covenant*, eds. E. Ulrich and J. VanderKam (Notre Dame, IN: University of Notre Dame Press): 91–101.

1994b '*Zab* Impurity in Qumran and Rabbinic Law', *JJS* 45: 273–78.

1995a 'A Fragment on Fetal Life and Pregnancy in 4Q270', in *Pomegranates and Golden Bells*, ed. D. Wright (Winona Lake, IN: Eisenbrauns): 445–48.

1995b 'The Red Cow Purification Rites in Qumran Texts', *JJS* 46: 112–19.

1999a 'The Purification Liturgies', in *The Dead Sea Scrolls after Fifty Years.* Vol. II, ed. P. Flint and J.C. VanderKam (Leiden: E.J. Brill): 202–12.

Eshel, E.

1997 '4Q414 Fragment 2: Purification of a Corpse-Contaminated Person', in *Legal Texts and Legal Issues: The Proceedings of the Second Meeting of the International Organization for Qumran Studies, Published in Honor of Joseph M. Baumgarten* (Leiden: E.J. Brill): 3–10.

Milgrom, J.

1994b '4QTOHOROT[a]: An Unpublished Qumran Text on Purities', in *Time to Prepare the Way in the Wilderness: Papers on the Qumran Scrolls*, eds. D. Dimant and L.H. Schiffman (Leiden: E.J. Brill): 59–68.

Qimron, E.

1991 'Notes on the 4Q Zadokite Fragment on Skin Disease', *JJS* 42/2: 256–59.

Translations

Charlesworth, J. *et al.*

1995 *The Dead Sea Scrolls: Hebrew, Aramaic, and Greek Texts with English Translations. Vol. 2: Damascus Document, War Scroll, and Related Documents* (The Princeton Theological Seminary Dead Sea Scrolls Project; Tübingen: J.C.B. Mohr [Paul Siebeck]; Louisville, KY: Westminster/John Knox Press).

Charlesworth, J. and E. Qimron

1994 *The Dead Sea Scrolls: Hebrew, Aramaic, and Greek Texts with English Translations. Vol. 1: Rule of the Community and Related Documents* (The Princeton Theological Seminary Dead Sea Scrolls Project; Tübingen:

J.C.B. Mohr [Paul Siebeck]; Louisville, KY: Westminster/John Knox Press).

Dupont-Sommer, A.
1961 *The Essene Writings from Qumran* (Eng. tr., G. Vermes; Oxford: Blackwell).

García Martínez, F.
1994 *The Dead Sea Scrolls Translated: The Qumran Texts in English* (Leiden: E.J. Brill).

Gaster, T.
1957 *The Scriptures of the Dead Sea Sect in English Translation* (London: Secker & Warburg).

Vermes, G.
1997 *The Complete Dead Sea Scrolls in English* (New York: Penguin Books).

Wise, M. *et al.*
1996 *The Dead Sea Scrolls: A New Translation* (London: HarperCollins).

Bibliographies

Fitzmyer, J.
1990 *The Dead Sea Scrolls: Major Publications and Tools for Study*, SBL Resources for Biblical Study, 20 (Atlanta: Scholars Press).

García Martínez, F. and D. Parry
1996 *Bibliography of the Finds in the Desert of Judah 1970–1995* (STDJ, 19; Leiden: E.J. Brill).

García Martínez, F. and E. Tigchelaar
1998 'Bibliography of the Dead Sea Scrolls', *RevQ* 18:459–90, 605–39.

Maier, J.
1996b *Die Qumran-Essener: Die Texte vom Toten Meer* (Uni-Taschenbücher (München), 1916; Basel: Friedrich Reinhardt).

Pinnick, A.
Weekly updated online bibliography of the Dead Sea Scrolls, 1995 to present, *The Orion Center for the Study of the Dead Sea Scrolls and Associated Literature Website*: http://www.orion.mscc.huji.ac.il.

Qimron, E. and J. Strugnell
1994 'Bibliography on the Halakha at Qumran', in *Qumran Cave 4 V: Miqṣat Ma'aśe ha-Torah* (DJD, X; Oxford: Clarendon Press): 124–30.

PART I

THE CONCEPT OF PURITY AT QUMRAN

1

INTRODUCTION

1. Purity in the Second Temple Era

The Second Temple period of ancient Judaism was marked by a heightened concern for purity. Issues of cult and purity engaged and divided Jews more in this period than at any other time in antiquity. Purity was not limited to a handful of extremists who lived in the desert, but was rooted at the heart of Jewish life. Although arguments continued over the degree of purity required, there was general agreement among Jews that purification was necessary not just for priestly figures but also for laity. The *Haberim*, who ate ordinary food in a state of purity, the *Therapeutae* and the Morning Bathers are a few examples of Jewish laity who held to strict purification codes. The Talmud contends that the purity of Temple vessels was more important to some priests than murder (b. *Yoma* 23b; y. *Yoma* 2.1). After the Temple's destruction in 70 CE, purity continued as a consolatory substitute for the Temple cult, but its religious grip gradually waned.

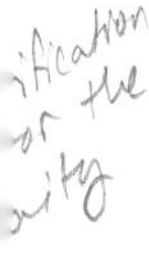

Purification in the Second Temple era was expected in a variety of situations. Many Jews purified before meals and before prayer. Jews regarded the city of Jerusalem as the holy city and purified themselves before participating in the festivals there. Priestly portions of the harvest were selected in a state of ritual purity. Initiations into various forms of Judaism were marked by purifications. Purity rituals preceded divine revelation (cf. *War* 2.159; Mt. 3.16-17). Immersion was required after ritual impurities and was sometimes a sign of atonement as well.

Among all of the Jewish groups of the Second Temple era, the Qumran Community was the most rigorous in the maintenance of purity. The laws of purity and impurity were a central concern for the authors of the Dead Sea Scrolls. In fact, the majority of the community's laws recorded in the extant manuscripts deal with matters related to the cult and purity. One

Scroll author states that it was due to improper cultic and purity practices in Jerusalem that he and others separated from the rest of the people (4Q394–99). The author pleads with his readers not to give in to those who would seek to conduct the cult according to a different calendar and a lower code of ritual purity. Several texts require purity of body as well as spirit in order to join the community, and individuals were ostracized during their times of impurity.

The sectarian emphasis on purity is supported by Josephus' descriptions of the Essenes and by the site at Qumran, where an ancient aqueduct connected many cisterns and immersion baths. In fact, Josephus' report on the Essenes is very close to the community documents of the Scrolls in the area of purity. For example, Josephus confirms that the sect required baths and a change of clothing before meals (*War* 2.129-31). The group at Qumran appears to have been a celibate, monastic group of Essenes who had separated themselves for a period of time (or a lifetime). Their mission was apparently the pursuit of divine revelation through the study of the Torah in preparation for the messianic age.

The most extensive parallel data on specific impurities come from Rabbinic literature. Even though the Mishnah was compiled some one and a half centuries after the demise of the sect, and the Talmud even later, many Rabbinic arguments reflect and clarify controversies found, explicitly or implicitly, in the Scrolls. Like the sectarians, the Rabbis regard the biblical laws of cult and purity as central to their ideology. However, while they share much in common with their ancient relatives at Qumran, they repeatedly adopt a more lenient stance in matters of impurity.

This volume collects the extant data of the Scrolls on purity and discusses them, in Part I, in terms of general concepts and available sources, and, in Part II, by particular impurities: corpse impurity, leprosy, bodily discharges and outsider impurity. Biblical, Rabbinic and other ancient Jewish texts will be utilized throughout to shed light on issues reflected in the Scrolls.

2. Definition and Description of Purity

Tohorah, purity, is a status achieved by both moral integrity and ritual purification, which is required of Israel in order for God's holiness to reside among and protect them (Num. 19.20; cf. Deut. 23.24). God promised to speak to Israel from his house, the Jewish Temple, and in particular from its inner room, the Holy of Holies (Exod. 25.22). In order to guard the holiness of the sanctuary, all Israel had to be pure before entering its courts. Purity restrictions were more severe the closer one was to the sanctuary. Only pure priests could enter the sanctuary. Levites maintained its courts and Israel could come and worship only in prescribed areas. It is important to note, nevertheless, that even when not going to the sanctuary, Israel had to maintain a certain level of purity in their homes, including, for example, bathing after sexual intercourse and menstruation, because of the presence of God among them.

Purity, *tohorah*, can be best understood in its relationship to, on the one hand, holiness, *qedushah*, and on the other, *tum'ah*, impurity. *Tohorah* is a state of being; it refers to the absence of impurity. Holiness, *qodesh*, *qedushah*, on the other hand, is an active force which comes from God. Holiness can be defined loosely as divine energy. At its core, holiness is another way of saying God, and indeed the favourite Rabbinic title for God is *Ha-Qodesh, Barukh Hu*, 'Holiness, Blessed Be He.' Qumran authors too use the word *ha-Qodesh*, the phrase *Qodesh Qodashim*, and sometimes just *Qodesh* as a synonym for God (1QS 10.4; 1QS28b 4.28; CD 6.1; 20.22) (Naude 1999: 192). Only God is inherently holy. Other persons and items can partake of God's inherent holiness only by extension and by divine designation. They can never be inherently holy, but they can mirror the divine holiness in various ways (cf. Lev. 11.44-45; 19.2-37). They imitate his otherness and separation from impurity, they strive for his perfection as far as possible, they exhibit the divine goodness (i.e. true justice and mercy), and they partake of divine power.

Holiness in Jewish tradition is composed of two major facets: one can be referred to in biblical terms, 'Consuming Fire', and the other is ethical goodness (Harrington 2001: 12–13). As 'Consuming Fire' holiness is that independent, separate ultimate power which reacts violently when coming into contact with any impurity or imperfection. This divine force is worshipped in other cultures as well. However, the second aspect of holiness, ethical goodness, in Judaism describes the quintessential nature of God and so it is part of what holiness means (Milgrom 2000: 1712). When an Israelite defrauds a fellow Israelite or simply withholds wages he is violating the command, 'Be holy as the Lord your God is holy' (Lev. 19.2).

As in other ancient cultures, holy persons and items in Israel are 'that which is unapproachable except through divinely imposed restrictions' or 'that which is withdrawn from common use' (Milgrom 2000: 1715). Separation from that which is opposed to God is necessary. The flip side of the coin is that the holy person is also separated *to* God, i.e. he or she is committed to emulating God's goodness. J. Naude, who has analysed the root *qdsh* in the Scrolls, concludes that an item which is *qodesh* is on the side of or within the realm of God (Naude 1999: 193). In this way, holy items are privileged; they partake of the divine energy and experience supernatural power (cf. Lev. 5.15-16). The holier the person, the more severe the restrictions but also the greater the benefit in terms of access to God, gifts and privileges.

More than anything else, purity is necessary for the activation of holiness (Exod. 22.30 [Eng 31]). In fact, in many biblical as well as Qumranic texts, the verb *lehitqadesh*, 'to sanctify', means to go through ritual purification (1QS 3.4; Exod. 19.10, 14; 2 Sam. 11.2, 4; Milgrom 1991: 965). Impurity of any kind, ritual or moral, can impinge on God's realm and bring destruction on the community (Milgrom 1991: 47). The priestly system of the Pentateuch labels as holy God's house and the priests, his agents, as well as all gifts brought to him, whether in the form of priestly food offerings or animal sacrifices. Some items are *qodesh qodashim* – holy of holies: God's inner sanctuary, the high priest who alone is allowed to enter it, and certain sacrificial offerings. All of the sanctuary space, personnel and offerings must be pure in order for the system to be effective.

Impurity, *tum'ah*, refers to those items which threaten the pure status of Israel and its sanctuary. The greatest impurity of all is sin, violation of God's law, and this must be expiated by repentance and animal sacrifice. However, many impurities are not due to transgression or rebellion but simply result from the human condition. As described in Leviticus and Numbers, impurity can be brought on by certain physical human processes, such as, death, leprosy and sexual discharges (see Table 1). Sometimes a disease, such as leprosy, may be inflicted by God on an individual as a punishment for sin. These impure conditions, however, are not usually seen as the result of sin. Ritual impurity is 'natural, more or less unavoidable, generally not sinful, and conveys an impermanent contagion' (Klawans 1998: 392–93); sin, on the other hand, brings permanent danger unless atonement is made. Moral impurity cannot be purified without repentance and sacrifice. Ritual impurity is easily purified by biblical prescriptions, usually involving bathing in water and the passage of time, but it can also be more complex, as discussed in the chapters below.

The Torah is insistent that ritual impurities must be purified (Num. 19.20) before the impure individual can participate in Temple worship, and specific purification rules are set forth. Impurity must be kept away from the sacred or it will endanger the entire community as God's wrath breaks out upon it. And, since ritual impurity is contagious, 'there is a danger that the contagion will spread throughout the community, thus effectively isolating the entire community from contact with God'

Table 1. Biblical Impurities and their Purifications

Impure Person	Duration	Purification
Severe Impurities		
1. Corpse (Num. 19)	always	non-purifiable
2. Leper (Lev. 13–14)	x + 8 days	1st day: spr, l, sh, b 7th day: sh, l, b 8th day: bird rite, sacr (3), d (2)
3. *Zab* or *Zabah* (person with abnormal genital discharge) (Lev. 15.3-15, 28-30)	x + 8 days	b, l, sacr
4. Parturient (Lev. 12.2-5)	boy: 7 + 33 days girl: 14 + 66 days	[b, l,] sacr
5. Corpse-impure priest (Ezek. 44.26-27)	15 days	[b, l, spr,] sacr
6. Corpse-impure Nazirite (Num. 6.9-12)	8 days	[b, l, spr,] sh, sacr
Lesser Impurities		
7. Corpse-impure layperson (Num. 11–18)	7 days	b, l, spr (2), eve
8. Menstruant (Lev. 15.19-24)	7 days	[b, l,] eve
9. One who emits semen (Lev. 15.16-18)	1 day	b, l, eve
10. Carcass-contaminated person (Lev. 11.24-40)	1 day	[b, l,] eve

Key
x indefinite; b bathing; l laundering; eve evening; sh shaving; spr sprinkling;
d daubing; sacr sacrifice; [ ] data assumed
For further references and explanation, cf. Milgrom 1991: 986–87

(Frymer-Kensky 1983: 403). Therefore, severe impurity bearers are banished from the camp or at least isolated.

The worst kind of reaction will occur if the two categories of holiness and impurity mix. Scripture warns that the one who brings impurity into contact with holiness will incur the penalty of *karet* (Lev. 7.20-21). T. Frymer-Kensky says *karet* brings 'calamity to his entire lineage through the direct intervention of God ... and without necessitating social action' and serves as a 'divine reinforcement of the boundaries between sacred and profane by providing a sanction for acts which violate these boundaries but which are not normally provided with legal sanctions' (Frymer-Kensky 1983: 405). Thus, even if done secretly, for instance, the unlawful mixing of holy food gifts with an impure liquid, will bring the wrath of God.

While it is a physical condition, ritual purity has little or nothing to do with hygiene. The Rabbis are careful to make a distinction between *tohorah* and *nekiyyut* (hygienic cleanness). In fact, after bathing in a muddy pool for ritual purification, people used to take an ordinary bath in drawn water to become clean (b. *Shab.* 14a). The 'ritual' in 'ritual impurity' is brought into relief when one realizes that it can be transferred to an individual who is simply in the same room as a corpse or a leper even where no physical contact has been made. Also, this impurity can affect houses and fabrics which have no connection to germs or disease. Furthermore, it only comes into effect when the priest pronounces it so. Most strikingly perhaps, the Torah does not address the impurity of Gentiles; apparently they do not biblically receive or convey ritual impurity (except the Gentile corpse, cf. Num. 31.19).

3. Purity in the Scrolls

The many purity texts found at Qumran reveal an approach to purity which is stringent. The biblical prescriptions for purity are often increased and impurity is regarded as a more potent force than it is by any other ancient Jewish group in antiquity. Although there are some differences between the texts, the similarity of the concept and laws of purity are more striking than the differences. Whatever is concluded about the identity of the writers, it must be conceded that their beliefs cohere, by and large, on the matter of purity. Thus, this book repeatedly refers to the 'sect' or the 'sectarian attitude' and takes seriously the claim of the Halakhic Letter (MMT) that the group departed from the priestly mainstream both ideologically and physically.

Scholarship on the Dead Sea Scrolls in the area of purity has been fertile. Rabbinic scholars immediately noticed parallels between the purity required by the sect and that required by the *Haberim* of Rabbinic literature. The Rabbis provide a developed system of purity and impurity in the Mishnah based on the laws of the Torah. Both the Rabbis and the Qumran sectarians looked to Scripture when determining the law. By comparing the Qumran data with the Rabbinic system, the stringent attitude of the sect comes into sharper relief.

In addition to the above general understanding of purity in Scripture, the Dead Sea Scroll community is known for a certain distinctive interpretation of purity: (1) among the Scrolls there is a tendency to expand the categories of holiness and purity of the Torah and to interpret purity restrictions maximally; (2) impurity is defined as a more malevolent force than in any other ancient Jewish text in terms of sources, contagion and purification; (3) the pure food and drink of the community, often called 'the purity', becomes a central focus of the community; (4) ritual and moral impurity are intertwined.

3.1. The Extension of the Concept of Holiness

The concepts of holiness and impurity described above are intensified by the Scroll authors. Classifications of purity in the Scrolls, while not always by the same author, reveal a broad congruence at least in concept. Scripture's categories are inevitably interpreted maximally. Let us examine this extension of levels of holiness and purity in the categories presented above: *qodesh qodashim* (holy of holies), *qodesh* (holy) and *tahor* (pure).

(1) *Qodesh qodashim*. According to the Temple Scroll, *qodesh qodashim* is not just one room in the sanctuary but the entire sanctuary, as well as the altar area, laver and stoa (11Q19 35.8-9). Personnel labelled *qodesh qodashim* include all priests, not just the High Priest (4Q397 6–13.4; 1QS 8.5-6; 9.2-8; cf. 4Q400 1.19) and can also refer to angels (Qimron and Strugnell 1994: 173).

Many of the texts make a distinction between the holiness of the community and the greater holiness of the priests within it. The Halakhic Letter states that all Israel 'are *qodesh*, holy, and the sons of Aaron are [most holy]' (4Q396 4.8, Qimron reconstruction). Whereas Scripture regards the priests as 'holy', the author refers to them as 'most holy' and the Israelites as 'holy' (cf. also 1QS 8.5-10; 9.6; 4Q381 76.7). The Community Rule refers to 'ranks' in the 'community of holiness' and describes two specific groups: a house of holiness (consisting) of Israelites and a *most holy* congregation (consisting) of Aaron (1QS 8.5-6; 9.2-6). The idea that the priests comprise the congregation of Aaron at the most holy level and Israelites are a holy community of perfection appears to be a hallmark of Qumran law and can be derived from Scripture (cf. Exod. 19.6; Lev. 11.44; 1 Chron. 23.13, Qimron and Strugnell 1994: 173). The Damascus Document distinguishes between those Israelites who live in a camp of 'perfect holiness', perhaps the Qumran Community, and those who live in the 'camps', perhaps Essenes living among the cities of Israel (Qimron 1992: 287–94). The text reports that the former were celibate and the latter had families (CD 7.4-7). Josephus may be referring to the same movement when he says some Essenes are celibate (*War* 2.120; *Ant.*

18.21), others are not (*War* 2.160). The excavations of the site at Qumran appear to support the celibate character of the community. The main cemetery appears to contain approximately 1200 graves of men only; 11 women and 5 children, possibly of more recent origin, are buried separately (Hachlili 2000: 662; Zias 1999).

(2) *Qodesh*. In spatial terms, the Scrolls expand the category of *qodesh* from the sanctuary to the entire city of the sanctuary, Jerusalem. According to the Halakhic Letter, 'Jerusalem is the camp of holiness and is the place which he has chosen from among all the tribes of Israel. For Jerusalem is the capital of the camps of Israel' (4Q394 3.10-13; cf. 2.16-18). The writer sets forth his hierarchy of holy space as follows: 'And we are of the opinion that the sanctuary [is the "Tent of Meeting"] and that Jerusalem is the "camp", and that "outside the camp" [is outside Jerusalem], that is, the encampment of their settlements' (4Q394 2.16-18). From these passages it becomes clear that the writer equates Jerusalem with the 'camp', i.e. the wilderness camp of Numbers. His respondent evidently disagrees and probably limits the application of holiness to the sanctuary only. The Temple Scroll too regards the entire city of the sanctuary as holy (11Q19 47.4).

Certain restrictions on Jerusalem preserve its sacred status. The Messianic Rule and the Temple Scroll both require at least a three-day purification for impure persons before entering into the sacred assembly or the holy city, respectively (1Q28a 1.25-26; 11Q19 45.7-12). These rules are probably patterned after the holiness restrictions on Israel at Mount Sinai where three days of purification were prescribed before God's holiness engulfed the mount (Exod. 19.10-11). The Temple Scroll bans the physically impaired from Jerusalem just as the officiating priests could not be in any way physically impaired (11Q19 45.12-14; cf. 1QM 7.3-5; 4Q394 3.19-20; 4Q394 4.1-4). Both the Temple Scroll and the Damascus Document prohibit sexual intercourse within Jerusalem (11Q19 45.11-12; CD 12.1-2). Hides used in Jerusalem must be from animals slaughtered as sacrifices within the city according to both the Temple Scroll and the Halakhic Letter (11Q19 51.1-6; 4Q397 2.1-4). To ensure the holiness of Jerusalem and its cult, dogs are banned from the city, holy food must not remain overnight, and the purity of liquids must be maintained so that water containers are not retroactively contaminated (4Q394 4.5-8).

While the sectarians' picture of Jerusalem may seem extreme it must be viewed in light of its Second Temple context in which there was a tendency to extend the holiness of the Temple outward (cf. Isa. 52.1; Joel 4.17). Certainly, before participating in festivals at Jerusalem Jews purified themselves (*Ant.* 14.285; Jn 18.28; m. *Hag.* 3.6; Büchler 1926–27: 23–24). Furthermore, Antiochus III upheld Jerusalem's claim to purity even in non-festival periods by forbidding impure animals or their hides to be brought into the city:

> ... King Antiochus 'also published a decree, through all his kingdom, in honor of the temple, which contained what follows: "It shall be lawful for no foreigner to come within the limits of the temple round about; which thing is forbidden also to the Jews, unless to those who, according to their own custom, have purified themselves. Nor let any flesh of horses, or of mules, or of donkeys, be brought into the city, whether they be wild or tame, nor that of leopards, or foxes, or hares; and, in general, that of any animal which is forbidden for the Jews to eat. Nor let their skins be brought into it; nor let any such animal be bred up in this city ... And he that transgresses any of these orders, let him pay to the priests 3000 drachmas of silver."' (*Ant.* 12.145-46 [12.3.4])

The point of Antiochus III's edict was to prevent the defilement, not just of the Temple, but of all Jerusalem.[1] This concern must have been widely supported by the general population in order for it to have elicited such a decree from the pagan king. Also, Josephus remarks on the purity of Jerusalem that persons with severe impurities, (for example lepers, persons with genital discharges) were excluded from the entire city (*War* 5.227-32; cf. m. *RSh.* 4.1-2; m. *Kel.* 1.6-9). Thus, the sectarians' attitude toward Jerusalem, although more restrictive than their contemporaries, reflects the spirit of the times. The unusual aspect is not the imputed holiness of Jerusalem but the degree to which Jerusalem should be set apart from other cities; i.e. how much purity should be required. —Imputation of Holiness

According to the sect, holy personnel include all of the community, not just the priests. In fact, the Qumran writers identify their community using the following terms: 'holy house for Aaron' (1QS 9.6); 'holy among all the peoples' (1Q34 3 ii 6), 'assembly of holiness' or 'holy community' (1QS 5.20; 9.2; 1Q28a 1.9, 13; 4Q181 1 ii 4); 'holy council' (1QH 15.10 [7.10]; 1QM 3.4; CD 20.25; 1QS 2.25; 8.21; 1Q28a 2.9); 'temple of men' (4Q174 1.6); 'the holy ones' (1Q33 6.6); God's holy people (1Q33 14.12), 'men of holiness' (1QS 8.17), 'congregation of the men of perfect holiness' (CD 20.2-7; 1QS 9.20); 'most holy dwelling for Aaron' (1QS 8.8). The community refers to itself as a group sanctified, or set apart, for Torah study in the desert (1QS 8.13-15). Each member is considered an *ʿish ha-qodesh*, 'a holy man' (1QS 5.13, 18; 8.17, 23; 9.8). Thus, the Qumran community regarded itself as, first of all, holy. The height of this

1. Yadin 1983: 240; to be sure, before its widening in the Hasmonean era, Jerusalem was no more than a sort of precinct of the Temple.

holiness seems to aspire to that of the angels, who are the usual referent of *qedoshim*, 'holy ones', in the Scrolls (Naude 1999: 189; Collins 1999: 613–14).

Since the community is a type of 'temple', made up of holy personnel, stringent purity laws come as no surprise. The sect clearly had a more intense notion of holiness as revealed by more purity restrictions than any other known Jewish group in antiquity. Candidates to the group were examined after one year for proper adherence to the sect's laws (CD 15.14-15). Even members of the larger non-celibate community are forbidden to marry Gentiles or even to accept their food (4Q394 1.6-11; 4Q174 1.4; cf. Deut. 23.2-42; *War* 2.409-10; opp. m. *Zeb.* 4.5). Some texts suggest that a truly pure person (*'ish tahor*) would not eat the contents of even a sealed vessel in the house of the dead, whereas the Bible allows this (4Q274 3 ii 4; 11Q19 49.8; Num. 19.15). And, the novitiate is not even allowed to touch an elder who would then become impure by the newcomer's lesser status of purity. Physically impaired persons, although not technically impure, were excluded from the entire community. They were considered a hindrance to holiness deterring the presence of the holy angels within the community (CD 15.15-16). As we examine the relevant Scriptural passages on the particular impurity matters below, it will become clear that the authors usually combine and harmonize Scripture's laws to the most rigorous interpretation.[2] J. Milgrom refers to this unique exegetical trait as 'homogenization' (Milgrom 1989a: 165–80). At times, the rules go beyond what Scripture requires by any stretch of the text.

The Scroll authors themselves admit that they are expecting a higher behavioural code than the simple intent of the law and there is a clear sense that not all of the sect are maintaining the same level of purity. Nevertheless, the texts advocate being *tahor yoter*, more pure (4Q274 3 ii 4). Sect members should strive to be the pure man as opposed to the

2. Baumgarten 1999b: 81, offers examples of the sect's 'leniency'. (1) vessels in a corpse-contaminated house are forbidden even if covered to the *tahor yoter*, but allowed to the general populace; (2) a man defiled by semen who has only one garment may wear it without washing it (4Q274 2 i 6-7); (3) the Qumran community did not always require immersion for purification; the verb *rahas* was interpreted sometimes as just washing (*ibid.*); (4) corpse impurity comes only from limbs of a corpse, not those amputated from a living person. Baumgarten's #1 is more strict than Rabbinic halakha which does not require anyone to eat the food within a sealed vessel; #2 Scripture does not require the semen-contaminated to wash his clothes, only bathing is necessary; #3 remains in the area of speculation, leaving only #4 as a clear-cut leniency.

ʿ*adam miYisrael*, the average Israelite (11Q19 49.8). Those truly seeking to please God will be more scrupulous than the letter of the law.

Some texts even offer a sort of mission statement. The Rule of the Blessings exhorts the community, '[. . . May you] dedicate yourself for the holy of holies, for [. . . you are made] holy for him, and shall glorify his name and his holiness' (1Q28b 4.28). The author envisions the sect as a worship community at the highest level of holiness. The Community Rule gives a rationale for its rules too and connects them explicitly with holiness. The writer places the concept directly in the metaphysical realm and exhorts Israel to live 'in accordance with these rules in order to establish the spirit of holiness in truth eternal' (1QS 9.3). The group is described as if it were a community of priests, all trying to exemplify the highest levels of holiness (Dimant 1986: 188). The levitical command, 'Be holy even as the LORD your God is holy' (Lev. 11.45) could be considered the group's motto.

Clearly, the Qumran sectarians were seeking to maximize their acquisition of holiness by the stringency of their laws. They took literally the divine vision of Israel in Exodus as a 'kingdom of priests, a holy nation' (Exod. 19.6). Their conviction was that as they strove to please God, he would bestow greater holiness upon them. They applied this principle not primarily in the ethical realm but in the ritual, focusing largely on diminishing ritual impurity as far as possible and on increasing cultic demands. In their view, God would be better served if all of the community adopted a stringent code of behaviour, both in the Temple and outside it, and strove for the ideal holiness, even pushing beyond the explicit requirements of Scripture.

A case in point is the issue of sexual intercourse. Marital relations were rejected at Qumran because they were regarded as a deterrent to holiness. Although the biblical laws are clear that celibacy is not the divine mandate on Israel, they are also clear that sexual intercourse causes impurity (Lev. 15.18; cf. Acts of Thomas 8: 'filthy intercourse' must be abandoned to be a 'holy temple', cited in Baumgarten 1990: 23 n 23). Thus, according to the Qumran reasoning, greater holiness is obtained if sexual intercourse is simply avoided. Unsurprisingly, even in the larger Essene community (I agree with those scholars who understand the Damascus Document as a text of a larger parent community of the sect, not just the group at Qumran), sexual intercourse was not allowed on the Sabbath, a period of holy time (Broshi 1992: 589–600).

The Rabbinic view, by contrast, is embedded in Deuteronomy. Here all of Israel are holy by divine designation and they are obligated to maintain that holiness by observing the law (Deut. 26.19; cf. also Deut. 7.6; 14.2, 21). The level of holiness is only that which the law demands. Compare this statement from *Numbers Rabba*: 'Be holy, for as long as you fulfil my commandments you are sanctified, but if you neglect them you become profaned' (*Num. R.* 17.6). Holiness is linked directly to the explicit laws of the Torah. Even a minimal interpretation, if it can be supported, will suffice. The Rabbis would stop with the laws as stated in the Pentateuch. The Qumran group, however, demands holiness as defined by the levitical priests and sometimes even beyond that.[3]

The category of holy food was expanded as well. Priestly food includes animal tithes, all fourth-year fruit, as well as gifts of birds, wild animals and fish (11Q19 60.3-4; 47.17; cf. 4Q396 3.2-4; Num. 31.28-29). By contrast, the Rabbis do not require any priestly tribute from birds, game or fish, and they allow farmers to eat their own animal tithes (after priestly portions are given) and fourth-year fruit (m. *Zeb.* 5.8; *Sif. Num.* 6[9]). Most strikingly, all slaughter within a three-day radius of Jerusalem had to be conducted at the sanctuary with substantial portions of each sacrifice given to the priests (11Q19 52.13-21; cf. Lev. 17.3-4). Levites too must be given sacrificial portions.

(3) *Tahor.* Jewish sites other than Jerusalem were considered to be at a lower level of purity, they were simply *tahor*, pure. The Temple Scroll states: '[And let] their cities [be] clean, *tahor*, forever, and the city, which I will hallow by settling my name and [my] Tem[ple within (it)], shall be *qadosh*, holy and *tahor*, clean' (11Q19 47.3-4; cf. 4Q394 2.17-18).

It may be that the residents of cities on the level of *tahor* would have been understood by the sect to refer to the Essenes living throughout Israel, not at Jerusalem. They were, of course, non-celibate and thus would not endanger the Temple-like status of Jerusalem. The community at Qumran, however, seems to regard themselves as a substitute for the Temple itself and thus proscribes sexual intercourse at Qumran. Nevertheless, the level of *tahor* is still quite stringent, including such purity laws as the prohibition of sexual intercourse on the Sabbath and the required ritual slaughter of fish.

3. Some strains, nevertheless, of the maximalist position are present in Rabbinic sources as well, for instance, the Talmud enjoins, 'Sanctify yourselves even in what is permitted' (b. *Yeb.* 20a). If you just follow the Torah you could still be a glutton, a drunk or full of animal lusts – restrain yourself. *Leviticus Rabba* states that even an unchaste look is to be regarded as adultery (*Lev. R.* 23 end). Similar ideas are presented in the ethical instructions of the Gospels (cf. Mt. 5.27). However, the maximalist position is not the norm in Rabbinic literature.

3.2. Levels of Impurity: Sources, Contagion and Purification

Impurity was the biggest threat to the group's holiness and hence its access to God. The War Scroll warns that priests will become defiled with the blood of the slain (1QM 9.8). The Damascus Document insists that Jews 'separate from all impurities according to their law and to let no man defile his holy spirit' (CD 7.3-4). Moral purity, as well as ritual purity, are essential to holiness. The Community Rule explains that stubbornness, lewdness and deceit are contrary to 'the fruit of holiness' (1QS 10.21-23; cf. 1QM 13.2-4; 1QS 8.11). Even the holiness of contributions from Israel to the priests is cancelled if the items were obtained in an unethical manner (CD 16.14, 16, 17; 4Q271 2 ii 14, 15).

The concept of purity at Qumran is more specifically defined by the sect's prescriptions and prohibitions with regard to impurity. Ritual impurity can be discussed in three categories: sources, contagion and purification. In all of these areas, the sect takes a maximalist approach to impurity, regarding it, more than any other ancient Jewish group, as potent and threatening (see Appendix B).

(1) *Sources.* The sect follows the Torah in regarding the following items to be sources of impurity: death, leprosy and sexual discharges. These impurities can be divided into major impurities, i.e. those which require multiple days of purification and various complex rituals, and minor impurities, which only last until sunset (cf. charts in Milgrom 1991: 986-91; Frymer-Kensky 1983: 400-401; Harrington 1993: *passim*).

In addition to these three major categories of impurity, the sect identifies two additional sources of impurity: outsiders and excrement. While the Torah does not include outsiders in its system of impurity, Jews in various periods did decree such defilement as a way to restrict contact between Jews and Gentiles (see Chapter 6). This is contrary to the standard Rabbinic position which accepts sacrifices from Gentiles, although this practice aroused controversy in the Second Temple period (m. *Zeb.* 4.5; cf. *War* 2.409-10).

Excrement is not included in the levitical purity laws as an impurity and the Rabbis make much of this omission. It once more reinforces the notion that ritual impurity is not a matter of hygienic cleanliness. Nevertheless, the filthiness of excrement is mentioned in Scripture in other contexts (cf. Ezek. 4.12-14; Zech. 3.3-4). More importantly, Deuteronomy requires the soldier to take care of this bodily function outside of the war camp on account of holiness (Deut. 23.13). Therefore, the sectarians, who regard themselves as a holy war camp (see below), add excrement to the list of impurities threatening the holiness of the community.

(2) *Contagion.* The above sources of impurity not only cause their bearers to be impure but, in many cases, also to be contagious to others. For example, Scripture states that the person who has become impure by contact with a corpse will transmit impurity by touch (Num. 19.22). A menstruant as well as her bed are impure and contagious to those who touch them (Lev. 15.19-22). Apparently, this secondarily contaminated person would have to perform a minimum purification of bathing and waiting for sunset. Contagion applies in every category of impurity as detailed in the chapters below.

The Rabbis rank the various sources of impurity according to their contagion potency and the types of purification needed to purify them (m. *Kel.* 1.3; m. *Zab.* 5.6-7), and there must have been a system of some kind at Qumran as well. The Temple Scroll reveals an intensification of contagion from either the biblical or Rabbinic systems. For example, those who have had sexual intercourse or a nocturnal emission must remain outside the sacred city for three days and bathe on the first and third days of their impurity (11Q19 45.7-12).

In addition to the biblical contagion laws, many Qumran texts indicate that impurity bearers are contagious to each other. In ordinary cities individuals afflicted with gonorrhea (*zabim*), corpse-contaminated persons, and menstruants are confined to separate dwellings for the time of their impurity (11Q19 48.13-17). In addition, a menstruant may not touch a *zab* (gonorrheic) nor anything the *zab* has touched or lain on. If she does, she must launder her clothes and bathe, *ratsaḥ*, and then she may eat (4Q274 1 i 4-5). Apparently, impure persons can become even more unclean if they do not keep away from other impure persons.

Some texts (cf. 4Q514 lines 4-6; 4Q274 1 i 9) require individuals who are impure for an extended length of time to wash in order to eat. They would, of course, still be impure and barred from the communal meal but they would be allowed to eat (Milgrom 1994a: 177; 1991: 975–76). The question remains, where did this food come from? According to Josephus, the sectarians were not allowed to eat food from outside sources (*War* 2.143-44).

Qumran texts seem to oppose anything but full purification of impure persons before participation in community activities (cf. also 4Q266 9 ii 1-4; 4Q277 1.13; 4Q394 1.17-19; 11Q19 51.2-5). The Pharisees ascribed to the *tebul yom* concept, according to which an impure person who had bathed would be allowed contact with all but sacred items, even though the time of purification was not yet completed. For example, the Pharisees would intentionally make the participants in the red cow rite impure so that they needed to immerse, to the dismay of the Sadducees, being in this intermediate status when they performed the rituals. In this instance, the Qumran sect would have concurred with the Sadducees.

Another salient feature of impurity in the Scrolls is its contagious effect on objects. For example, the house of death contaminates everything within it, from locks and lintels to floors. This contrasts markedly with the Rabbinic view that only the items specifically mentioned in Scripture (Lev. 11.32-33; Num. 31.20-23) are susceptible to impurity: persons, rinsable vessels (e.g. copper pots), earthenware, utensils and clothing. Nevertheless, Scripture does say that *kol*, 'everything', within the house of death becomes impure (Num. 19.14). The sectarians do not limit the context of that 'everything' as the Rabbis do. Stone can be susceptible as well as wood and even dust (11Q19 49.12-16; CD 12.16).[4] According to Rabbinic interpretation, earthenware is exempt from impurity on the outside of the vessel, perhaps because earthenware is porous and can absorb unclean substances even when washed. The sectarians regard even the glazed exterior of earthenware to be off limits to the scrupulously pure person (Maccoby 1999: 77).

(3) *Purification.* Purification can take place, according to the Torah, by means of water ablutions, the passage of time, and, for the most serious impurities, rituals involving blood. Blood rituals are of various types: the most powerful are the sacrifices upon the altar. Only these can expunge impurity resulting from various sins as well as from leprosy, gonorrhea and extensive female blood flows resulting from childbirth or disease.[5] Also priestly purifications often require this powerful purgation (cf. Ezek. 44.26-27). Lesser, routine impurities such as menstruation and corpse

4. Cf. H. Eshel 2000: 45–52, who limits the susceptibility of stone vessels at Qumran to those which contain oil stains. As support for this idea he cites 11Q19 49.12 which refers to the 'defiling smirch of oil', CD 12.16 which singles out oil stains as conveyors of impurity, and Josephus' statement that Essenes scoured their skin of oil so as not to become impure (*War*. 2.123). The Mishnah mentions stone and earth as insusceptible and wood is susceptible only if it forms a complete vessel (m. *Kel.* 2.1; m. *Oh.* 5.5). A biblical source for the idea that stone and dust are susceptible might be the fact that stones of leprous houses along with their dust are impure and must be discarded (Lev. 14.40-43).

5. Milgrom, 1989b: 103, points out the moral and ritual uses of purification sacrifices in the Torah: 'The *ḥatta't* ... which purges the sanctuary of its physical impurity (Lev. 16.16) is also prescribed for the elimination of moral impunity (Lev. 16.21). Indeed, this purification offering is required whenever any of the Lord's prohibitive commandments are violated (Lev. 4.2) and, according to a variant priestly tradition (Num. 15.22-31), it is mandated if any commandment, permissive or prohibited, is disobeyed.'

contamination require a week of separation and purification. Corpse contamination is distinctive because it requires the sprinkling of special purification water, *me niddah*, the mixture of the ashes of a red cow mixed with water, red wool and hyssop on days three and seven of the purificatory week. Other impurities such as sexual intercourse or handling a carcass require only a bath and a wait of one day.

J. Baumgarten offers the interesting possibility that *me niddah* was used to purify other impurities, both ritual and moral, in addition to corpse contamination (Baumgarten 1999b: 83-87). He derives this notion from the mention of *me niddah* in 4Q512 for those 'impure of many days' (not just those contaminated by a corpse), as well as the implication in 1QS 3.7-9, where *me niddah* seems to remove moral impurity (also cf. 4Q277 1.2). He also notes various biblical contexts, in addition to those about corpse impurity, where *me niddah* is used, for example the inauguration ceremonies of priests and Levites (Lev. 8.1-36; Num. 8.7). The priests performed specific purification rituals involving blood, oil and water, and the Levites were sprinkled with *me hatt'at (= me niddah)* before initiation. Perhaps these rituals were a model for the priestly Qumran sect. On the other hand, perhaps there really was an ancient procedure whereby a penitent was sprinkled with *me niddah*. The Psalmist pleads, 'Purge me with hyssop and I shall be clean' (Ps. 51.9). Hyssop is one of the few ingredients of *me niddah*. In any case, even if *me niddah* was required of all serious impurity bearers, the more usual cleansing by immersion in water would undoubtedly have been required too, as it was of the corpse-contaminated person (Num. 19.19; 4Q277 1 ii 8-10; cf. also the semen-impure of Lev. 15.13).

Purifications prescribed by the Scrolls generally intensify the biblical instructions. As a minimum purification from any impurity, apparently, laundering, bathing and waiting for sunset were required (4Q396 4.1; 11Q19 50.8-9). Only clean water could be used for purification and it had to cover the entire person (4Q267 17.8-9).[6] An immersion pool which is too shallow is invalid for purification (CD 10.11-13). The Rabbis require only bathing as a minimum purification; a person who has immersed is granted access to everything in the profane sphere and waits for sundown only to gain access to sancta.

The Scrolls tend to focus not on the purification system as a whole but

6. Opp. Baumgarten's suggestion that because the semen-impure may stand in the water and drink (CD 11.1), he is not required to immerse (1999b: 91). Rather, he must be completely covered with water, even if he has to bend down and stand up again (cf. CD 10.10-11). 4Q414 requires both sprinkling and immersion (cf. also 4Q513).

on polemics, distinctive views of the sect that set them apart from the reigning cultic establishment in Jerusalem. Thus, the insistence on full purification, including a wait until sunset on the following day, takes up an inordinate amount of space in the texts. The sectarians required immersion for ritual impurity as well as moral impurity. Sinners were instructed to immerse in water in order to be purified. In fact, all their belongings were impure too (1QS 5.20; cf. 1QpHab 8.3-3). However, without repentance immersion was meaningless (1QS 3.3-9; 5.13-15). The same view is endorsed by both John the Baptist, who immersed repentant sinners (Mt. 3.6-11), and Philo of Alexandria (*The Unchangeableness of God*, 7–8). A blessing marks the end of the purification period (cf. Baumgarten 1992b: 202, for Rabbinic parallels). The person who has been purified may now effectively pray to God.

3.3. The Tohorah of the Community

Among the Scrolls, *tohorah* takes on a distinctive meaning and refers to the pure food and drink, and sometimes other property, of the community. In Scripture, pure food can refer to (1) animals permitted for food as well as (2) food which has been kept from impurity. For example, it is forbidden to eat pork because the pig is an impure, forbidden animal (Lev. 11.7), but even lamb, which is permitted, becomes forbidden if it comes into contact with impurity (Lev. 7.19-20; 11.1-45). For the sectarians, not only are biblically impure animals avoided but the category is expanded to include bee larvae and water creepers; ritual slaughter is extended to include insects and fish (CD 12.12-15). With regard to pure food, the larger issue at Qumran, there seems to be a twofold concern: (a) to keep the food pure for its own sake, and (b) to avoid personal contamination by eating impure food. Below, we will discuss the ritual purity of food and then the contagion power of liquids.

(1) *Food.* The Rule of the Community describes the standard of purity which was in practice at Qumran. Ordinary food was eaten in a state of purity, that is, communal food, the *tohorah*, was harvested, stored and eaten in a state of purity; all members had to bathe before eating it (1QS 5.13; cf. *War* 2.129). According to other sources, members wore white before eating the meal and no physically impaired person could partake of it (*War* 2.129-131; *Ant.* 18.21; 1Q28a 2.3-10; cf. 1Q33 7.4-6). Even discarded animal bones were protected from contamination. They were put in jars so dogs could not get to edible remnants and contaminate them. Qumran is clearly concerned about the purity of the food for its own sake. An individual had to be completely pure to eat of the *tohorah*; a

person whose purification was in process could not join the others at the communal table or even touch pure food (4Q514 line 4; cf. 4Q274 2 i).

Candidates for membership in the community were put on probation and examined for a whole year before they were allowed to eat the communal food; at least two years of probation were necessary in order to drink communal liquids (1QS 6.17-21; *War* 2.138; cf. CD 15.14-15). Food could also be contaminated if a transgressor ate of it (see below under Moral and Ritual Impurity). Members who violated community rules were excluded from the table (1QS 7.2-21; 8.22-24; *War* 2.143).

In addition, there was concern over the defilement of a pure person through eating impure food. A prime example is the insistence that food in sealed vessels in the house of a dead person be avoided (11Q19 49.8; 4Q274 3 ii 4). The concern was not to protect the food, which was already considered impure, but the individual.

Food terms reinforce the distinction between priest and Israelite. The food of the laity is called *tohorat ha-rabbim*, the pure (food) of the many (1QS 6.16-17, 25; 7.3) or *tohorat 'anshei ha-qodesh*, the pure (food) of the holy persons (1QS 5.13; 8.17). However, *tohorat ha-qodesh*, the pure sacred food, required greater sanctity (Milgrom 1991: 975). The mixture of ordinary food with priestly food is said to result in *ʿavon zimmah*, the 'sin of immorality' (4Q513 11.3). Moreover, Ordinances B states that if a priest marries a Gentile, his entire family is forbidden to share his food, i.e. the food given him by Israel for his family (4Q513 11.3; cf. 4Q398 4.10-11).

Did the Qumran sect think their communal meals were sacrifices, *qodashim*, or even non-sacrificial priestly gifts, *terumah*? On the one hand, food was treated with the respect and careful handling the priests gave to the sacrifices. They were not allowed to come into contact with impurity. On the other hand, there were laity among the sect who would not have been allowed to eat sacred food. When the Temple would be restored according to their views, the sect believed it would be able to reinstate the entire cultic system of Scripture, but for the time being the regimen of the sect would have to suffice.

The *yaḥad's* insistence on eating in purity reminds one of other Jewish groups in antiquity, especially the *Ḥaberim*. The *Ḥaberim*, often translated the 'Associates', were early Rabbinic sages who insisted on eating ordinary food in a state of purity just as the priests ate the sacred food in purity. Some Rabbis forbade causing any impurity to the ordinary food of the Land of Israel, since the entire land retains a certain measure of holiness (b. *Sot.* 30b; b. *Git.* 53a; b. *AZ* 55b; b. *Nid.* 6b; Maccoby 1999: 158). The prevailing view was that it was not forbidden but it was praiseworthy not to cause impurity to ordinary food. To be sure, the

Torah requires priestly agricultural offerings to be free of impurity. The *Haberim* could be counted on to separate these priestly dues from the crops in a state of purity.

The Gospels too support the notion that many observant Jews purified themselves before eating. Mark says the Pharisees washed their hands before eating and that this was a 'tradition of the elders', i.e. it was passed down from earlier generations (Mk 7.3). In fact, he claims that the concern to wash cups, pitchers and kettles was prevalent among all the Jews. Even if this is an exaggeration, the reference is clearly not just to priestly food (cf. also Mt. 23.25). Luke states that it was Pharisaic practice to bathe completely before eating (Lk. 11.38). Thus, like the Qumran sectarians, many Jews of the Second Temple period ate ordinary food in a state of purity.[7] Even Jews in the Diaspora washed before eating (Regev 2000a: 229).

Is there an exegetical base for these laws and practices? In their effort to require maximal purity at Qumran, it seems that these sectarians combined the purification rules addressed to all Israel in Leviticus 11–15 with the purity required to eat sacrificial portions in Leviticus 7.19-21. As a result of this 'homogenization' came the requirement that all Israelites (even those hopelessly impure) bathe before eating any food.

(2) *Liquid.* Liquids are the conveyors of impurity par excellence according to the sectarians and the Rabbis. In fact, food is not susceptible to impurity when dry. Liquid not only receives but also transmits impurity to other items (CD 12.16-17). If liquid is pouring out of a vessel onto an impure item, that impurity can be transmitted by the flow upwards back into the vessel (4Q394 3.5-8). The analogy of impurity and physical dirt gives force to the role of liquids as conveyers of impurity. Just as dirt is transferred from one item to another by liquid, so metaphysical impurity too is conveyed by liquids.

According to Qumran texts (4Q284a; 4Q274), crops which have been wetted in any way, even by rain or dew, become susceptible to impurity (Baumgarten 1994a: 109-23). Food for the communal meals had to be pure from the time of harvesting to the point of consumption. Even the juice of grapes or olives in the harvesters' baskets could ooze out and

7. Cf. m. *Hul.* 2.5 which discusses the purity of eating certain game (those from which blood did not exude) with dirty hands, the assumption being that most ordinary food would have to be eaten in purity. Also m. *Zab.* 3.2 and t. *Miq.* 6.7 assume a certain standard of pure food for non-priests, cf. Harrington 1995: 42-54; S. Spiro 1980: 186-216; Judg. 12.7-9.

convey impurity to the produce.[8] In order to ensure that the whole process of harvesting is done in purity, some texts insist that neither unclean persons, purifying persons, nor those who are not full members of the sect may harvest produce, lest their impurity be transferred by moisture to the produce (4Q284a 1.2-8; 4Q274 3 ii 7-9).

The original Scriptural basis for this issue must be Leviticus 11.38 where it is stated that if water 'is put', *yutan*, on seed and a carcass falls on it, the seed becomes impure. Thus, liquid conveys impurity to produce. According to the 4QTohorot texts, however, the possibility of impurity being conveyed to the fruit began already when the harvesters gathered the fruit into their baskets. Juice could seep out in the process and, according to the sectarians, convey any impurity with which it might come into contact.

A similar concern over the purity of liquids is attested in other contexts and in other documents from Qumran. As we have seen already in the Damascus Document, oil stains in the house of the dead had to be removed so that corpse impurity would not spread (CD 12.15-17). The Temple Scroll insists that all liquid, even water stains, in such a house becomes impure and must be removed (11Q19 49.8-11). Perhaps the most striking rule showing concern for liquids is that access to communal drinks was granted to the novitiate at Qumran only after two to three years of probation (1QS 6.20; 7.20; cf. *War* 2.123).

A look at Rabbinic laws regarding liquids will provide more information, at least as a parallel case. According to the Mishnah, impure items will render food and hands impure at the first degree if they are moist (m. *Makh.* 1.1; 6.4-5; m. *Ter.* 11.2-3; cf. *Sif. shem. sher. par.* 8.1). However, the interpretation of Leviticus 11.38 is not as stringent as among the sectarians. On the basis of the word *yutan*, 'is put', the Rabbis insisted that there must be intentional and desired putting of the water on the seed by permission of the owner in order for it to become susceptible to impurity (m. *Makh.* 1.1; 2.3-4; 3.6; 5.11; 6.8; b. *Qid.* 59b); the Schools of Hillel and Shammai discuss the matter. The issue of purity of the harvest was important to the Sages too and they quarantined the workers of the olive presses while they pressed the oil (m. *Toh.* 9–10). However, it was only at this stage, when liquid was pressed from the fruit, that impurity was allowed to become an issue. Also, unlike the Qumran sect, the Rabbis limited the issue to certain crops, for example grapes, olives.

8. It is interesting that the Rabbis define the liquid of Lev. 11.34 as seven particular liquids, none of which is fruit juice. It may be a matter of economics: if all fruit juices were susceptible, this would require purity of all fruit harvesters just like those who harvested olives and grapes.

The Qumran texts mention harvesting other crops in purity as well, for example figs, pomegranates (4Q284a 1.4). The Mishnah tractate Tohorot is concerned that the *ʿam ha-ʿareṣ*, the ordinary Jew who could not be trusted to keep purity codes, or Gentiles, will touch and defile pure items.

The sect allows produce to be placed in a natural stream or pool of water for protection from impurity. Complete immersion in the water will provide protection. For example, if herbs are harvested in excess of what can be sold or consumed immediately they could be stored in a collection of water and thereby rendered insusceptible to impurity. The Mishnah records examples of this kind of protective measure. For example, lupines placed in a *miqveh* are not considered susceptible because they are *completely* wet (m. *Makh.* 4.6). The Sages considered fig-cakes which had been placed under water to be valid as well (m. *Makh.* 1.6).

(3) *Ritual vs. Moral Impurity*

One of the most distinctive features of the Qumran literature is the link between purity of body and spirit. While the two categories are more or less distinct in the Hebrew Bible, and definitely so in Rabbinic literature, in the Scrolls the line between ritual and moral impurity is blurred. According to Josephus, the elders of the Essene community, those at the top of the ladder of moral integrity, are also those most susceptible to ritual impurity. Apparently, as one matures in moral character, sensitivity to impurity increases. Novitiates to the sect are not allowed to touch the elders or the pure food of the sect, lest they contaminate them. The Community Rule states that new members are cleansed by their humble repentance as well as the sprinkling of cleansing waters (1QS 3.6-9). The impurity of leprosy is referred to as the work of a malevolent spirit, not just a condition in need of the prescribed purifications of Lev. 14 (4Q272 1.1-16). The gonorrheic, like the leper, is considered a sinner, his condition brought on by lustful thoughts.[9] According to the Damascus Document, the word of a transgressor is not believed until the person has been ritually purified (CD 10.2). Violators of any of the sect's laws become impure and are excluded from handling or eating the community's pure food lest their impurity defile the meal (1QS 5.14).[10] In a word, moral failure causes ritual impurity.

Both physical and moral frailty is the lot of human beings according to

9. This stands in contrast to the Rabbinic insistence that the *zab*'s condition did not result from sexual stimuli, see Baumgarten 1999b: 88.

10. Even if an individual is accused of a crime by only one witness, that is enough to exclude him from eating the pure food of the community (CD 9.23; cf. Deut. 19.15), Wacholder 1989: 174.

the Scrolls. There is a sense throughout these texts of the inability of human beings to maintain proper standing before God. Humanity is by nature subject to frailty and impurity, and one's best efforts to please God often fail miserably, requiring that continuous penitence be undertaken. The body is as much of an obstruction as one's wayward spirit. According to the Scrolls, the human being is a 'creature of clay, fashioned with water, foundation of shame' (1QH 9.22) and a 'corrupt man and a foundation of wicked flesh'. The author of the Community Rule confesses, 'I belong to evil humankind to the assembly of wicked flesh; my failings, my transgressions, my sins ... with the depravities of my heart belong to the assembly of worms and of those who walk in darkness' (1QS 9.9-10).[11] According to the Community Rule, Israel and its land require continuous atonement (1QS 5.6; 8.6-7; cf. CD 14.18). Whether the impurity flows from the body or results from violations of the law, it excludes individuals from the presence of God. Nevertheless, while members struggle with innate impurity, whoever does not join the sect is hopeless: 'Defiled, defiled shall he be' (1QS 3.4).

This general sense of human inadequacy before God is heightened at times of impurity as revealed in the penitence of purifying persons even though no specific sin is mentioned. The blessing recited by the purifying person in the Community Rule reveals that the individual is keenly aware of his sinful condition but trusts in God's ultimate goodness to show him mercy, 'In his great goodness he atones for all my iniquities. In his righteousness he cleanses me of the impurity of the human and [of] the sin of the human being, in order [that I might] praise God [for] his righteousness, and the Most High [for] his glory' (1QS 11.14; cf. also 4Q512 39 ii). The purifying person thanks God for setting up a way of dealing with impurity so that an impure person can come back into the worship community. Any kind of impurity, large or small, moral or ritual, is believed to hinder a person's prayer, thus the purifying individual blesses God and acknowledges human shortcomings. In one text the purifying person asks purification 'from all *'ervat basarenu*', probably a non-moral physical impurity (4Q512 36-38 iii). Another general purification occurs before festivals. Here the purifying person asks for grace for all of the hidden acts of guilt (inadvertent sins) (4Q512 34 v). In 4Q512 29-32 vii 9, there is a clear mixture of ritual and moral impurity concerns. The unclean person thanks God for (delivering) him from *pesha'* (sin) and for

11. P. Sacchi 1979: 26–27, says the Qumran sect makes an 'identification of man and impurity'. According to F. García Martínez and J. Trebolle-Barrera, the sect regards the human being as a 'structure of sin', (1995: 155). For Sacchi, the Scrolls regard impurity as 'not only a force which weakens man, [but also as] evil itself'.

purifying him from ʿ*ervat niddah* (some type of impurity). In another fragment, the purifying person confesses outright, 'I sinned' (4Q512 28 viii). Several columns contain a serious note of contrition as purifying individuals give thanks to God for purifying them and making them a holy people.

It seems to be a fair statement that at Qumran, the purifying person, no matter what the impurity, is going through moral renewal as well. That is, as he purifies his body, the individual also examines his soul. According to the sectarians, the human being, trapped as he is in a morally unreliable body, is always dependent on God's grace and must constantly make sure he is in favour with God. Unwitting sin plays a strong role in Qumran doctrine as well as in the Torah and its Rabbinic interpretation. The sectarians state unequivocally that if sin of any type is present, all the waters in the sea will not be effective in removing a person's impurity, even if it is simply one of the normal processes of the body (1QS 3.4-5). Ritual purification was not automatic with ablutions but was made possible only by God's grace; only the pure in heart could enter the waters and become completely pure. For the sect, all types of impurity were part of the same conceptual framework; that is, all types of impurity in some way tainted a person and required penitence of him as well as ablutions.

The notion that ritual impurity bars a person from God's presence, no matter how great or slight the impurity, and that it forms a barrier which must be removed, is a biblical principle (Num. 19.20). Purification was necessary before participating in Temple worship and before any of the sacred festivals. Before holy events, such as the Sinaitic revelation, all Israel were required to purify themselves (Exod. 19.10-11). Now that the sanctuary and its feasts were on hold, purification seems to have been even more essential to the sect to make up for this spiritual gap. Just as ritual purity prepared biblical Israel for holy events and Temple entry, it was considered necessary at Qumran for bringing the presence of God into the community (Maccoby 1999: 212).

The Scrolls require ablutions before prayer, whether entering the Temple or not (4Q414 2 ii 5-6; 4Q512 42–44 ii). The blessing is given while standing in the water (cf. Mt. 3.16-17). According to Josephus, the Essenes used a loincloth in the water to maintain modesty (*War* 2.161; 4Q512 11 x 4). Apocryphal books support the notion that without ritual purity one's prayer to God will not be accepted. In the Testament of Levi (2.3), before Levi prays that the Lord make known to him the 'spirit of holiness', *to pneuma to hagion*, he is obliged to bathe. According to other texts, immersion was required before one could pray for forgiveness (Life of Adam and Eve 6–7; Sib. Or. 4.165-68).

The Bible connects ritual impurity and moral impurity in several contexts. The term, *niddah*, menstrual impurity, is used, especially by the prophets, to describe the sin of Israel (for example Isa. 30.22). Likewise, Ezekiel speaks of sprinkling pure water on wayward Israel to purify her of sin (Ezek. 36.25). The Psalmist uses the language of corpse impurity, in his confession of guilt as he pleads, 'Purge me with hyssop, and I shall be clean', referring no doubt to the hyssop used to cleanse a person from corpse contamination. Did sinners use hyssop and the ashes of the red cow in their atonement process or is this only a metaphor? (Cf. Baumgarten 1999b: 84). Ritual purification did, at least on occasion, accompany repentance; for example, Jacob required his entire family to undergo ritual purification when they repented from idolatry (Gen. 35.2).

Nevertheless, to say that the Qumran sect made no dichotomy between ritual purity and purity in the ethical sense is an oversimplification of the matter. The sect was reading the biblical text too carefully not to notice the distinctions present for different types of impurity, and certainly moral transgressions carry punishments in addition to ritual obligations. It would be more accurate to say that there is at times a blurring of the line between the two types of impurity, and both require ritual purification.

The notion that physical, ritual impurity is connected to moral, inner impurity was sorely opposed by the Rabbis, who kept ritual impurity in the area of natural processes without moral overtones. The famous story of Yohanan ben Zakkai's conversation on the subject with a pagan illustrates the tension (*PRK* 4.7). A pagan came to Rabban Yohanan ben Zakkai and asked why Jews use the ashes of a red cow to purify the corpse-contaminated person. Ben Zakkai explained that an impure individual is a person possessed of an evil spirit, and for support he quoted Zechariah 13.2 where God promises to chase all spirits of impurity out of the land. This seems to reflect a popular notion in antiquity (among both Jews and pagans): impurity was a demon which had to be exorcized. The pagan was satisfied with ben Zakkai's answer, but the Rabbi's disciples were aghast for it was completely contradictory to what they had been taught. Their teacher mollified them by explaining that his answer was addressed to the pagan, who would only be able to understand the issue in such terms; to them, however, he confirmed his belief that the red cow rite, and by implication all of the impurity laws, are observed by Jews simply because God had so commanded, and these laws had nothing to do with evil spirits. Even leprosy and gonorrhea, which the Bible does sometimes associate with sin, do not represent an invariable connection between the disease and the moral condition of the afflicted person (see Chapter 4). Nevertheless, the Rabbinic story corroborates the popular notion that ritual impurity was the work of an evil spirit.

4. Archaeology

The archaeological record supports the heightened concern of the texts in regard to ritual impurity both at Qumran and throughout the Land of Israel during the Second Temple period. Two major types of finds related to purity concerns are *miqva'ot*, ritual immersion baths, and stone vessels, i.e. those insusceptible to impurity.

4.1. *Miqva'ot*

The excavation of the Upper City of Second Temple Jerusalem yielded a remarkable number of ritual baths. According to N. Rosovsky:

> At least one *miqveh* – 'a collection [of water]' – and often more, was found in every house in the Herodian Quarter. Most common among the many kinds of ritual baths was a rock-cut stepped pool, its lower part covered with a gray plaster ... the Palatial Mansion, the largest house discovered in the Upper City, contained two especially large ritual baths; each had two doorways, located side by side, so that the bather could enter through one before purification and, once cleansed, leave through the other. At times the steps were separated down the middle by a low wall, creating one path for going down to the water, another for emerging. (Rosovsky 1992: 31)

While many of the users of these *miqva'ot* would no doubt have been priests, who were obliged to maintain a higher standard of purity, it is significant that there was a *miqveh* at every single home. Evidently, many non-priests too felt it necessary to have a private *miqveh*. In addition, ritual baths have been found in Galilee, certainly for the use of non-priests. Some of those uncovered were attached to synagogues in several sites, such as in Herodion and Gamla (Reich 1987: 205–12). Ritual purification, then, was a concern which affected both priests and non-priests throughout the land of Israel and especially in Jerusalem.

At Qumran an aqueduct connects ten purification installations. Six of these show strong technical similarities to the above *miqva'ot* in Jerusalem (Reich 2000: 729–30). A staircase runs the entire width of the *miqveh* as opposed to the narrow staircase carved into the side of the installations found in Jericho. In both the Upper City homes and at Qumran, these stepped baths cover 15–17 per cent of the entire area; this large number of purification installations reflects the daily life of a priestly community, or at least one committed to the maintenance of ritual purity. As the priests purified before eating the holy portions (Lev. 7.19-21; b. *Ber.* 2b), so the Qumranites too bathed before meals. In fact, the *miqva'ot* at Qumran are much larger and would have been able to accommodate the many sectarians who would have needed to bathe at the same time before the communal meal.

Ritual baths have also been found adjoining cave-tombs in this period. An enormous cemetery dating from Hasmonean and Herodian times (seven miles long over seven hills) has been discovered outside the town limits of Jericho, in accord with Jewish law which stipulated that burials should be situated at least 50 cubits outside of a town (m. *BB* 2.9) (Hachlili 1979: 28). *Miqva'ot* have been found also at cemeteries in Judaea: (1) at the tombs of Helena of Audubon, and (2) in the courtyard of a burial cave at Jericho (Kon 1947: 31–38; Reich 1980: 251–53; Hachlili and Killebrew 1983: 112). These facilities enabled corpse-contaminated persons to complete a degree of purification immediately so that they could return to their daily affairs (see Chapter 3 below). Since it is not explicitly prescribed in Scripture, the provision for an immediate ritual bath for corpse contamination reveals the concern of Jews in the Second Temple period to purify as soon as possible from impurity, and even when not going to the Temple or handling sacred items.

Need for Quick Purification

The provision of a purification installation outside the community for the use of purifying individuals is apparent at Qumran as well. While the various cisterns and *miqva'ot* are centrally located, one installation is located outside of the site at the place where the aqueduct enters the area. R. Reich suggests that this *miqveh* was used by those who were impure and therefore forced, at least temporarily, to leave the premises (Reich: 2000: 730–31). Thus, if an individual had to bury the dead or simply relieve himself, he could leave the camp to do so and then purify himself before his return. Indeed a pool is located next to a large room on the east side of the camp which was tentatively identified by R. de Vaux, recently supported by J. Magness, as some type of toilet (Magness 2000: 715–16).

Archaeologists note a decline in the number of ritual baths after the destruction of the Temple (Regev 2000a: 235 n 35). Thus, from the evidence of the *miqva'ot*, purity concerns seem to have been at a peak during the Qumran era.

4.2. Stone vessels

According to Jewish law, stone is insusceptible to impurity. It is not in the list of susceptible materials in Lev. 11.32-33; in fact the text explicitly states that cisterns are insusceptible to impurity (Lev. 11.36). Some scholars suggest that stone vessels are insusceptible because they are 'entirely from unworked material' (Regev 2000a: 230). In any case, since stone is insusceptible to impurity, both impure and pure persons can use the same vessel and not be concerned about the transfer of impurity. Even

Called stone Jars

if an impure (dead) insect or carcass comes into contact with it, a stone vessel is still eligible for use since it cannot receive impurity.

The most important type of stone vessel is the *kallal* (*calyx krater*), the large jar used for storing food and liquids. It was used by the rich and required a complicated production technology due to its large size and decorative rims. John mentions six large stone vessels for Jewish purification rites, each holding 20–30 gallons (Jn 2.6) used for a wedding at Cana in the Galilee. These were no doubt *kallal*-type vessels (Regev 2000a: 232). In the Upper City of Jerusalem, Y. Magen has discovered a cave used as a workshop for the manufacture of stone vessels (Magen: 1988).

More significant than the *kallal*, at least for this study, are the stone measuring cups discovered in settlements outside Jerusalem, because they cannot be connected with priestly matters or pilgrimage during festivals. Many of these stone cups were found in the Judaean hill country, Judaean Desert, Samaria, Galilee, the Golan Heights and the Transjordan. As E. Regev says, 'These finds attest that many Jews in smaller towns and the rural settlements actually maintained ritual purity ... Enormous number of vessels ... found in almost every known Jewish settlement in the Land of Israel, even the smallest ... For example, in Iotapata (Iodphat), the Galilean town which Josephus claims fortified itself against Vespasian in 67 CE, at least 120 fragments of stone vessels were found' (Regev 2000b: 232). These are not storage vessels but 'small domestic mugs, pitchers, and bowls that contained drinks and food for daily meals'. If these were just for storing priestly contributions, larger vessels would have been needed. This wide distribution of common vessels for cooking and eating made from stone reflects the 'everyday and common character of this maintenance of purity' (Regev 2000b: 233). It is important to note that archaeologists found this multiplicity of stone vessels during the Herodian period, the latest being found during the Bar Kokhba revolt. Thus, it is in the Qumran era that a concern with stone vessels and purity in general is most apparent.

Significantly, 200 fragments of stone vessels have been found at Qumran (Regev 2000a: 234). Although Qumranites certainly regarded stone to be susceptible to impurity, H. Eshel has claimed that this susceptibility was limited only to those vessels coming into contact with oil (11Q19 49.11-16; CD 12.15-17; cf. *War* 2.123; H. Eshel 2000: 45–52, see above 'Liquid'). Further archaeological support for purity at Qumran lies in the possible evidence of storage jars containing animal bones (see Appendix to Chapter 3, below; Magness 2000: 714). In sum, the archaeological data from both purification installations and food vessels found at Qumran supports the witness of the Scrolls that a sectarian community with a high standard of purity lived there during the Second Temple period.

5. Rationale and Significance

The biblical impurity laws have generated a fair amount of curiosity concerning the rationale behind them. Why were certain conditions considered impure? What is the connecting thread, if there is one, between the various impurity laws? Why was the matter of impurity so central in the Second Temple period, especially at Qumran?

5.1. Biblical Rationale

Ritual purity is first of all a marker separating Israel from non-Israel. This can be detected in the broad rationale that the Bible provides for its pure-food laws:

> 'I am the Lord your God who has separated you from other people. You shall therefore make a distinction between pure animals and impure, between impure birds and pure, and you shall not make yourselves abominable by animal, or by bird, or by any kind of living thing that creeps on the ground, which I have separated from you as impure'. (Lev. 20.24b-25)

Thus, by keeping the biblical purity laws, Israel was set apart from other nations. The people's lifestyle was different even down to the food they ate. Exodus 34.15-16 points out the danger in eating the food of non-Israelites: this social intercourse would undoubtedly lead to intermarriage between Israelites and pagans. To counter this possibility, the food laws so restrict the Israelites' diet that they cannot easily socialize with outsiders. If Israelites cannot eat with non-Israelites, they will not marry non-Israelites or be influenced by idolatrous practices, all of which entail pagan rituals and feasts in honour of the gods (Milgrom 1993: 282–83; Hayes 1999: 13, 35–36). Thus, the pure-food laws mark Israel as different than other nations and put into place barriers obstructing intercourse between them.

In addition to being a general marker between Israel and non-Israel, is there any further reason for these particular purity laws? Why these restrictions and not others? Biblical scholars have recently propounded the theory that the biblical impurity laws have a common thread which is symbolically important. Together they emphasize the separation of life and death, and mark Israel as a people of life who shun those who associate with death. The most impure item in the system is the corpse, and it cannot be purified. Lepers, with their flaking skin and open sores, visually illustrate the process of decay and could be called living corpses.

Carcasses too cause impurity. Impure animals, most of which are carnivorous, convey contamination only when they are dead. Even the discharge of genital fluids may represent death, since there is a loss of life-giving forces.

By labelling contact with dead items impure, biblical authors may be emphasizing that Israel worships a living God, not a lifeless image. Yahweh is, rather, the giver of life, and the dead cannot praise him (Ps. 115.17). That which is dead is not part of the worship community, and those who associate with the dead, for example necromancers, are to be eradicated from Israel. In addition, the Torah promises that curses and death are the lot of a disobedient Israel, while an obedient people are sure to inherit blessings and life (Deut. 30.15-20). Hence, what is associated with death must be avoided and restricted because it is incompatible with the holy God who gives life. The Rabbis associate idols with the impurity of the dead and mark even further the distinction between lifeless gods and the creator of life (m. *AZ* 3.6; b. *AZ*). Those who must of necessity contact death, e.g. to bury their parents, must perform the necessary duty and then purify themselves before returning to the community of the living.

Further afield, the link between purity and life is also a non-Jewish phenomenon. In Egypt the hieroglyphs 'life' and 'happiness' flow from the purification flasks which purify the king. So also purification of the dead brings ritual purity and new life (Ringgren 1986: 288).

Nevertheless, some scholars have rightly raised the question, what do processes such as sex and menstruation have to do with death, given that they are necessary for life? Why are these bodily discharges defiling? How can semen, which produces life, be related to death? Some, as noted above, have suggested it is because such discharges are important life-giving fluids, and that loss of them, e.g. during sexual intercourse and menstruation, consequently means the loss of life (Milgrom 1991: 733). Furthermore, impurity emphasizes the mortality of human beings. To be human is to be susceptible to impurity, to participate in processes which generate life but always ultimately end in death, in other words, to be finite (Biale 1995: 147; Eilberg-Schwartz 1992: 31; Wright 1992: 729–41). God, the source of life, does not participate in this life–death syndrome. He is holiness itself, perfect and inherent. Humans are commanded to imitate his holiness, but because of their mortal frailty, they can never fully realize it. They must strive for it, however, by doing the works of the law and walking humbly before God. A standard of purity, both moral and ritual, which will activate God's holiness in Israel is the weapon human beings have against the powerful enemy of impurity, and represents the only way to neutralize it.

The Temple, God's house, must be kept free of this closed system of life processes doomed to decay and death. When entering the Temple, one enters God's realm, which is not subject to human limitations. As one scholar put it, 'The resting of the Divine Presence must be protected from mortality. When entering the Temple, one is entering the domain of eternity' (Maccoby 1999: 207). Similarly, at Delos, the sacred island of the Greeks, neither births nor deaths were permitted (Thucydides 3.04).

Anthropologists concur that the human body is often symbolic of the community at large. Restrictions on the body often reflect the community's view of cosmic boundaries. In this case, Israel has put a cordon around death, so to speak, by restricting the community's contact with those persons and items which are exposed to it. In this way the community associates itself with life.[12] Those who are involved with organic processes or are at the margins of death and life are in a liminal state and must perform prescribed rituals to re-enter the community (Douglas 1966: 53; Frymer-Kensky 1983: 400). The parturient, for example, is giving birth; in that process, however, she and her unborn child approach the dangerous boundary of life and death. Indeed, in the ancient world many women died in childbirth. Therefore, the parturient must go through a period of transition and purification before she can re-enter the community. Additionally, Israel's identification with life is especially significant, since many of her pagan neighbours ascribed to a cult of the dead (Wold 1979: 18).

Thus, there is a tension between life and death in the human being that God has nothing to do with. He is completely outside the realm of organic processes. As Leslie Cook puts it, 'purity is essentially a statement of difference: in having a body, the human being is radically different from God. The human being is subject to impurity; God is not' (Cook 1999: 48).

5.2. Qumran Rationale

In addition to the above rationale for the biblical purity laws, what do the Qumran texts themselves reveal about their rationale? It should be noted that the above association of impurity with mortality and death is supported by the Scrolls. Joseph Baumgarten notes several instances: (1)

12. The biblical laws concerning blood support the community's emphasis on life. According to the Noah story, 'Only the flesh with the life thereof, which is the blood thereof, shall ye not eat' (Gen. 9.4). According to Lev. 17.11, blood represents life and, even more, atonement for sin. The blood of an animal represents the life which it is forced to give up when it is offered for the sins and impurities of Israel (Cook 1999: 46).

Scale disease and death are associated, as noted above, in the Damascus Document where the 'dead' skin of the leper blocks the blood which carries the 'spirit of life'; (2) *zab* impurity is compared to corpse impurity: the *zab* 'may not eat just as if he were defiled by a human corpse', and touching the *zab*'s bed is directly compared to corpse impurity (4Q274 1 i 7-9; 4Q278); and (3) corpse impurity is juxtaposed with other impurities (4Q277) and Baumgarten goes so far as to suggest that the *me niddah* used for corpse purification may have been prescribed for all purifications (Baumgarten 1999b: 86–87). However, why are the Qumran laws so much more stringent than their biblical and Rabbinic counterparts?

As discussed above, the primary difference between the Qumran and biblical purity codes is the stringency of the Qumran laws and their close association of ritual and moral impurity. At Qumran, at least by contrast to biblical as well as later Rabbinic thought and practice, there is an extension of the whole concept of holiness and impurity. What is the reason for this? The answer lies in the realization that the Qumran community was (1) a priestly community composed of many priests and priestly sympathizers; (2) an apocalyptic community expecting the final confrontation between good and evil; and (3) a community seeking ongoing, new revelation from God. In all three cases a strong foundation of purity was seen as a necessary prerequisite.

The sect's knowledge of priestly matters and concern about current priestly practice reveal that it was composed of many priests as well as laity (Schwartz 1992: 229–40). The responsibility of the priests, first and foremost, was to ensure the sanctity of the sanctuary and implement its cult. The greatest threat to the sanctuary was not physical assault from outside but impurity resulting from within Israel. The priests had to be sure God was pleased with his house or else he might depart, leaving Israel defenceless or, worse, he might go to war against her (4Q267 2.8-9). Hence, ambiguity in the Torah was settled by the stricter interpretation. Also, many of the laws imposed on the community were in fact required for priests on duty in the Temple. Since the community was a substitute for the Temple, the sectarians tried to enforce these laws among themselves. Most Rabbis, by contrast, were laity. While they were very concerned about purity matters, as one look at the Mishnah will confirm, their interpretation usually reflects a bias in favour of the laity. Purity tends to be defined minimally compared to what is reflected in the Scrolls.

As many scholars have pointed out, initially based on 4QFlorilegium's *miqdash 'adam*, 'temple of human beings', the community itself was apparently considered a substitute for the Temple, at least during this period of exile in the desert (4Q174 1.6; cf. 1QS 8.5-9; 9.3-6). According to this text, the community is like a Temple and the study and practice of the law are substitutes for sacrifices: 'And he commanded to build for himself a temple of human beings, to offer in it before him the works of the Law.' Just as impurity defiles the Temple, so it now defiles the entire community and the community must be protected at all costs. The Temple is kept holy by physical purification as well as blood atonement. After the break with the Temple, the community is seen as a substitute and must be protected just as the Temple was. Levels of purity in the community parallel levels of purity required in the Temple and in the holy city.

The source for these stringencies can be found in Scripture. The Torah's wilderness camp (Exod. 19; Num. 5) or war camp (Deut. 23) are the possible models for the Qumran sect (cf. 11Q19 51.5-10). In these 'camps' purity is at a premium. No person contaminated by a corpse was allowed to remain within the wilderness camp (Num. 5.2). The three-day encampment at Sinai was without any marital relations. The Israelites purified their bodies and clothes in preparation for the holy encounter with God at the mountain. Similarly, the Deuteronomic purity laws for the Israelite troops were strict. No sexual relations were allowed, and even latrines had to be constructed away from the military camp. Here the reason is given, namely that the Holy One who fights Israel's battles will be mightily present among the troops and he should not be offended by the sight of any impurity. This powerful divine presence was the desiderata of each of the sectarians. Some texts refer to the holy angels being present among the community, every effort being made to keep the latter's high level of purity so that the angels would remain.

The wilderness camp of the Torah was constructed around a central sanctuary; thus the camp had to be as free of impurity as possible. In fact, Numbers 19 insists that remaining in impurity is a sin and requires an atoning sacrifice. All of the people are holy to some degree and impurity cannot be allowed to remain among them indefinitely (Num. 19.20). Similarly, for the sectarians in the context of the Second Temple period, all of Jerusalem functions like that holy wilderness camp.

As is evident in the chapters below, many laws simply reflect, not a paranoia of breaking the law, but a distinct effort to create more purity and holiness for their own sake; for example, the ritual slaughter of fish (CD 12.13-14), the prohibition of disabled persons from the holy city (11Q19 45.12-14; 1QM 7.3-5; MMT B 42–57), and bathing before meals (1QS 5.13). Although the Torah requires only holy food to be eaten in a state of purity (Lev. 7.19-20), the sectarians required even hopelessly impure persons to wash before eating their profane food (4Q274) (Milgrom 1994a: 177). Apparently, the Qumran group rejected marital relations (11Q19 45.11-12; CD 12.1-2), even though the holiest person in biblical Israel, the high priest, was a married man and the succession of the priesthood depended upon his marital relations (Qimron 1992: 291–94).

Anthropologists have demonstrated that in a period of persecution a group will reinforce its boundaries and increase its purity laws. In the period of the Second Temple it seems that the crisis in Judaism brought about by Hellenization increased emphasis on both apocalypticism and purification on the part of pious Jews (García Martínez and Trebolle Barrera 1995: 140). The rededication of the Temple by the Maccabees is described as a 'purification of the Temple' and their conquest as a 'purification of the land' (1 Macc. 13.48).

In addition to the overall Hellenistic crisis, the Qumran group did not enjoy the support of most Jews. The group at Qumran certainly were not in control of the existing cult at Jerusalem, and Israel at large did not agree with their understanding of purity. Especially in an unvalidated minority group, such as the Qumran sect, there is a strong concern to maintain distinct boundaries, and these often surface in the form of pure–impure restrictions on the body (Douglas 1966: 124; 1975: 269). What is allowed into the group is carefully monitored and the members tend to adopt rigid behavioural standards. Anthropologists claim that this is characteristic of fanatical religious groups. Outsiders too are sometimes considered contaminating. This reinforces the separation of sectarians from all others and preserves group identity (see Chapter 6).

The sect's apocalyptic character fits with its emphasis on purity and holiness for the following reasons. First, purity is necessary for holiness, and holiness fights wars. God can deliver his people from danger because he is holy (Exod. 15.11). The apocalyptic Qumran authors were expecting an imminent eschatological finale in which they, the minority group, were going to face all outsiders in a battle between the Sons of Light and the Sons of Darkness. Holiness, or the 'holy name', in some texts, would bring victory. According to the War Scroll David conquered the Philistines by means of the holy name (1QM 11.3; cf. 1 Sam. 17). The Damascus Document claims that the *yaḥad* will be safe because it takes refuge in the holy name (CD 20.34). Scripture is clear that purity must obtain in the War Camp (Deut. 23) in order for God's holiness to fight Israel's battles (Deut. 23.14). Like the holy war camp which the Israelite soldiers had to leave in order to relieve themselves, so the *yaḥad* had to keep impure bodily functions away from the community at Qumran. Recent archaeological studies confirm that no women were allowed at Qumran, just as no women were allowed to be priests in the Temple (Zias 1999). When the end is around the corner, life's normal routine is put on hold since it probably will not matter anyway. In order to win this eschatological confrontation, the Qumran writers insist, the highest level of purity possible will be necessary (Baumgarten 1996: 18). The holy angels are believed to be present among the community, and they will function as warriors in this final battle. The army of God (11Q13 2.9), they are exalted as the triumphant host of God over Belial (1QM 12.1-8). At the same time, they participate in the community meetings (11QBer 1.13-14; 11Q19 51.8, 10). The angels cannot tolerate impurity or defect; no physically impaired persons will be able to fight in the eschatological battle, and no impure persons, for example menstruants, can mingle within the holy camp (4Q274 1 i 6; 1Q28a 2.5). Humans and angels combine their worship together in the liturgies (4QShirShab and 4QBerakhot). The following statement expresses the level of holiness desired: 'Among the sevenfold purified, God will sanctify unto himself a sanctuary of eternity and purity among those who are cleansed, and they shall be priests, his righteous people, his host, and ministering (with) the angels of his glory' (Baillet 1982: 237). Thus, purity must apply in order for sectarians and angels to join in worship of God and aid the sect in battle (Naude 1999: 189; Davidson 1992: 132–242; García Martínez 1988: 118).

Secondly, the desired power of holiness purifies evil. According to the Community Rule, only the spirit of holiness can actually cleanse the sinner from his 'spirit of impurity' (1QS 4.20-21: one is purified 'by the holy spirit from all works of wickedness'; cf. 1QH 16.12). The 'spirit of life' is the only thing that can counteract the deadness of leprosy (4Q268; 4Q272). Mercy comes via the holy spirit (1Q28b 2.24). When the chosen ones become a foundation of the holy spirit they collectively will be able to atone for sin (1QS 9.3). The holy spirit is powerful and keeps the Instructor from erring (1QH 15.7 (7.7)).

Finally, the Qumran Community considered itself a recipient of ongoing divine revelation. It is well known that the sectarians' primary function was studying and copying Scripture. According to the Community Rule, they studied one-third of every night (1QS 6.7). The group's writings reveal that revelation was not limited to the existing Hebrew Bible but included their sectarian works as well. Again, holiness is necessary, for it is the vehicle for divine revelation. The prophets spoke by the holy spirit (1QS 8.16; cf. 2 Pet. 1.21). Similarly, the sectarians regarded their interpreters of prophecies as 'visionaries [*ḥoze*] of truth' (1QH 2.15); but considered the interpretations of all others, who do not interpret 'by the holy spirit', as 'visionaries [*ḥoze*] of deceit' (1QH 4.10) and 'falsehood' (4.20). The holy spirit reveals those who are the elect to specially chosen anointed individuals (CD 2.19). The Instructor is advised by the holy spirit (1QH 20.12 (12.12)). Unlike the Rabbis who see

Scripture as a special, closed revelation, the Scroll authors emphasize that revelation is, in J. Baumgarten's words, 'a continuing process involving a constant search for new illuminations' (Baumgarten 1977: 29–31). The Teacher of Righteousness was expected to present new revelation (1QS 8.12ff; CD 3.13ff). In order for the community to receive new revelation, holiness had to be at a maximum level, for only in a holy community could God be revealed. As explained above, holiness does not work without purity.

Mere study and observance of the law was insufficient to bring new revelation from God. For that, more holiness was required, and the only way additional revelation could be given was in the same manner that the original Sinaitic revelation was given, i.e. through a state of purity (Wacholder 1983: 16). Purity of both body and soul are required. At Sinai Israel refrained from sexual intercourse, set up boundaries upon the holy mountain, and performed special purifications. Moses was in such a state of holiness that he did not even eat or drink for 40 days, and when he returned to Israel, his face glowed with God's glory. Under these exceptional conditions, revelation was given and could be given again. Josephus states that the Essenes required ritual purification as a prerequisite to prophecy (*War* 2.159; Baumgarten 1999a: 207).

In conclusion, the Qumran sectarians were attempting to live at a high level of religious purity so that divine holiness could endow them with both revelation and power. Holiness was that divine energy that could protect, sustain and enhance the community. The Torah pointed the way to holiness and the purity necessary to activate it. It defined holy personnel, holy area, holy objects and the restrictions that guarded them. The priestly laws of the Torah were the link to divine holiness. Laws restricting the holiness of priests were often applied to the community at large since observance of them could channel in greater holiness. Other laws regarding holiness and purity were interpreted stringently and even augmented at times in order to intensify the level of holiness within the community, and ultimately, establish a closer connection with God.

This world-view explains somewhat the difference between the sect's purity views and those of the early Rabbis. The sectarians close ranks against all outsiders and the inner hierarchy is marked by stringent, ritual purity barriers. The Rabbis try to tame impurity even more than Scripture, and they compartmentalize ritual and moral impurity into separate categories. The Qumran sect regards the human being more holistically. The physical affects the moral well-being of a person. Just as a priest must be physically whole to serve in the holy courts, so the community must be whole. Impurity is a cancer that threatens a person's standing within the holy courts. While the Rabbis leave most matters of purity for the priests to take care of at the Temple, the Qumran community does not have this luxury. They *are* the Temple, and a vulnerable one at that, for they consist of human beings with immoral tendencies and impure bodily functions. One works through the other. For example, lust can cause impurity of the body. The Rabbis try to reduce the paranoia which can result from this kind of thinking. Rather than have a community which is always trying to achieve a status of perfection that will enable the angels to be present among them, the Rabbis agree to live on earth as limited mortals. They recognize that the human condition with its weaknesses is actually what makes possible the continuance of Israel. Each one is born in impurity but God is not offended by this; he is present at every birth regardless of the impurity the mother sustains.

The study of purity in the Scrolls is especially important for scholars in the fields of the Hebrew Bible, New Testament and early Rabbinic Judaism. Not only was purity central at Qumran but it was a core component of most early Jewish groups. Christianity is somewhat of an exception emphasizing moral but not ritual purity. Although apparently an observant Jew, Jesus appears to marginalize the whole issue of ritual purity by teaching that only what comes from a person's heart will defile him (Mt. 23.25; Mk 7.14-23; Lk. 11.38-40). In fact, Mark states that Jesus declared all foods clean (Mk 7.19). According to John, purity comes by association with Jesus (Jn 13.10; 15.3). The author of Hebrews, too, regards the physical cult and its purity laws as replaced by the work of Jesus. (Heb. 10.1-25).

Further Reading

On purity in ancient Judaism

Douglas, M.

1966 *Purity and Danger* (London: Routledge Press).

1993 *In the Wilderness: The Doctrine of Defilement in the Book of Numbers* (Sheffield: Sheffield Academic Press).

Frymer-Kensky, T.

1983 'Pollution, Purification, and Purgation in Biblical Israel', in *The Word of the Lord Shall Go Forth: Essays in Honor of David Noel Freedman in Celebration of His Sixtieth Birthday,* eds. Carol L. Meyers and M. O'Connor (Winona Lake, IN: Eisenbrauns): 399–414.

Harrington, H.

1995 'Did the Pharisees Eat Ordinary Food in a State of Purity?', *JStJud* 26: 42–54.

2001 *Holiness: Rabbinic Judaism and the Graeco-Roman World* (London: Routledge Press).

Hauck, F. *et al.*

1964–76 '*Katharos*', in *Theological Dictionary of the New Testament*, Vol. III, ed. G.W. Bromley (Grand Rapids, MI: Eerdmans): 413–31.

Klawans, J.

2000 *Impurity and Sin in Ancient Judaism* (Oxford; New York: Oxford University Press).

Licht, J.

1965b '*Qodesh, Qadosh, Qedushah*', in *Entsiqlopedya Mikra'it*, VII, eds. E. Sukenik and M.D. Cassuto (Jerusalem: Bialik Institute): 44–62.

Maccoby, H.

1999 *Ritual and Morality: The Ritual Purity System and Its Place in Judaism* (Cambridge: Cambridge University Press).

Milgrom, J.

1989b 'Rationale for Cultic Law: The Case of Impurity', *Semeia* 45: 103–109.

1991 *Leviticus1–16*, The Anchor Bible 3A (Garden City, NY: Doubleday).

2000 *Leviticus 17–22*, The Anchor Bible 3A (Garden City, NY: Doubleday).

Neusner, J.

1994 *Purity in Rabbinic Judaism* (Atlanta: Scholars Press).

Regev, E.

2000a 'Non-Priestly Purity and Its Religious Aspects according to Historical Sources and Archaeological Findings', in *Purity and Holiness*, ed. Poorthuis (Leiden: E.J. Brill): 223–44.

2000b 'Pure Individualism: The Idea of Non-Priestly Purity in Ancient Judaism', *JStJud* 31/2: 176–202.

Wright, D.P.

1992 'Unclean and Clean (OT)', in *Anchor Bible Dictionary*, Vol. VI (New York: Doubleday): 729–41.

On purity in the Dead Sea Scrolls

Baumgarten, J.M.

1967 'The Essene Avoidance of Oil and the Laws of Purity', *RevQ* 6: 183–93.

1990 'The Qumran-Essene Restraints on Marriage', in *Archaeology and History in the Dead Sea Scrolls*, ed. L.H. Schiffman (Sheffield: JSOT Press): 13–24.

1992a 'The Disqualifications of Priests in 4Q Fragments of the "Damascus Document", a Specimen of the Recovery of Pre-Rabbinic Halakha', in *The Madrid Qumran Congress*, II; STDJ 11; (eds. J. Trebolle-Barrera and L.V. Montaner; Leiden: E.J. Brill): 503–13.

1992b 'The Purification Rituals of DJD 7', *The Dead Sea Scrolls: Forty Years of Research*, eds. D. Dimant and U. Rappaport (Leiden: E.J. Brill): 199–209.

1994a 'Liquids and Susceptibility to Defilement in New 4Q Texts', in *The Community of the Renewed Covenant*, eds. E. Ulrich and J. VanderKam (Notre Dame, IN: University of Notre Dame Press): 91–101.

1999a 'The Purification Liturgies', in *The Dead Sea Scrolls after Fifty Years*, Vol. II, eds. P. Flint and J.C. VanderKam (Leiden: E.J. Brill): 202–12.

Dimant, D.
1986 '*4QFlorilegium* and the Idea of the Community as Temple', in *Hellenic et Judaic: Hommage à Valentin Nikiprowetzky*, ed. A. Caquot *et al.* (Leuven-Paris: Editions Peeters): 165–89.

Eshel, E.
1999 'Ritual of Purification', in *Qumran Cave 4 XXV: Halakhic Texts, Discoveries in the Judaean Desert XXXV* (Oxford: Clarendon Press): 135–54.

Eshel, H.
2000 'CD 12.15–17 and the Stone Vessels found at Qumran', in *The Damascus Document: A Centennial of Discovery*, ed. J.M. Baumgarten *et al.* (Leiden: E.J. Brill): 45–52.

García Martínez, F.
1988 'Les Limites de la Communauté: Pureté et Impureté à Qumrân et dans le Nouveau Testament', in *Text and Testimony: Essays in Honou of A.F.J. Klijn*, ed. T. Boarda *et al.* (Kampen, Netherlands: J.H. Kok): 111–22.

García Martínez, F. and J. Trebolle-Barrera
1995 *The People of the Dead Sea Scrolls* (Leiden: E.J. Brill).

Harrington, H.
1993 *The Impurity Systems of Qumran and the Rabbis* (Atlanta: Scholars Press).

Lieberman, S.
1952 'The Discipline in the So-Called Dead Sea Manual of Discipline', *JBL* 71: 199–206.

Milgrom, J.
1989a 'The Qumran Cult: Its Exegetical Principles', in *Temple Scroll Studies*, ed. G.J. Brooke (Sheffield: JSOT Press): 165–80.
1990b 'The Scriptural Foundations and Deviations in the Laws of Purity of the Temple Scroll', in *Archaeology and History in the Dead Sea Scrolls*, ed. L.H. Schiffman (Sheffield: JSOT Press): 83–99.

Naude, J.
1999 'Holiness in the Dead Sea Scrolls', in *The Dead Sea Scrolls after Fifty Years*, eds. P.W. Flint and J. VanderKam, Vol. II (Leiden: E.J. Brill): 171–99.

Qimron, E.
1992 'Celibacy in the Dead Sea Scrolls and the Two Kinds of Sectarians', in *The Madrid Qumran Congress: Proceedings of the International Congress on the Dead Sea Scrolls, Madrid, 18–21, March 1991*, Vol. I, eds. J. Trebolle-Barrera and L.V. Montaner (Leiden: E.J. Brill): 287–94.

Talmon, S.
1994 'The Community of the Renewed Covenant: Between Judaism and Christianity', in *The Community of the Renewed Covenant*, eds. E. Ulrich and J. VanderKam (Notre Dame, IN: University of Notre Dame Press): 3–24.

2

SOURCES

1. Introduction

The Scrolls found at Qumran reveal a surprising amount of congruence on the subject of purity. Although these documents represent differences of authorship, date and genre, they consistently champion a stringent standard of ritual purity. This emphasis on purity is supported by Josephus' descriptions of the Essenes and by the site at Qumran, where an ancient aqueduct connected many cisterns and immersion baths. The cemetery at the site appears to contain men only, and concurs with the claim of the texts to encourage Jewish men to take on a vow of celibacy and commit themselves to the study of Torah. Away from society at large, stringent standards of purity could be more easily maintained.

Comparison of the Scrolls with Rabbinic literature brings into relief the unique ideology of the Qumran texts (see Appendix A). The Rabbis of the Mishnah, successors to the Pharisees, often hold the views the Scrolls condemn (see Appendix B). Having chosen to remain within society, the Rabbis adopt a more moderate interpretation of Scripture than the Qumran authors.

The diversity of the Qumran texts may show stages of development or it may have resulted from disagreements within the Qumran community itself. While a diachronic approach seems healthy, we can only guess at the dates of many of the texts. It is often assumed that the Damascus Document and the Temple Scroll may be parent texts of the Qumran community, i.e. they were important to the sect but written earlier than its formation. Miqṣat Ma'aśe ha-Torah represents an early stage in the development of the sect before a full split was made. The Community Rule and related documents are written with a more acerbic tone against the opposition, and detail rules for a separate organization. Beyond these broad strokes, it is difficult to outline a diachronic development of purity laws in these texts. Many fragments from Cave 4, for example, contain a large amount of purity data but no context to help scholars ascertain their dates.

While it is unwise to regard all the Scrolls as coming from the same group of people, it is also not prudent to consider them simply as a batch of unrelated texts. As the survey of sources below will reveal, despite the differences a certain stance toward purity can be detected. As S. Talmon states: 'No other faction of Judaism at the turn of the era ... bears upon itself the stamp of facts welded with fancy, and of a hyper-nomism wedded with a fervent messianism' (Talmon 1994: 24). This 'hyper-nomism' is nowhere more evident than in the laws of purity. The group apparently took upon itself to become a surrogate Temple maintaining holiness at a level above the stated requirements of the Torah. Indeed, the sect sought continual revelation in its study sessions, during which purity was required at a high level so as not to offend the divine presence.

The approach in this chapter will be to survey particular Qumran texts and highlight the contribution of each to the subject of sectarian purity. In this process repeated elements in the purity data at hand will be noted in order to bring into relief the large amount of congruence among the Scrolls in the matter of purity. The implicit recurring questions will be, what purity data does each text provide, where do the texts stand in common and does this commonality stand in contrast to other ancient Jewish norms of purity?

The Scrolls most relevant to this discussion can be reviewed in the following categories: (1) Damascus Document (CD a+b, 4Q266–72; 5Q12, 6Q15); (2) Temple Scroll (11Q19); (3) Miqṣat Maʿaśe ha-Torah (4Q394–99); (4) Community Rule (1QS) and Related Documents; (5) Tohorot (4Q274, 276–78); and (6) Other Cave 4 Texts.

2. Damascus Document

The Damascus Document, also called the Zadokite Fragments, was first published by Solomon Schechter in 1910 from two medieval manuscripts found in a genizah in Cairo. In recent times Cave 4 at Qumran has yielded several more manuscripts (4Q266–73; 5Q12; 6Q15) which either parallel or add to Schechter's document. The oldest of these fragments dates back to the early first century BCE and the original text was probably composed near the end of the previous century (Baumgarten 2000: 169).

The work is a sort of legal treatise in two parts. The first section, the 'Admonition', details the pre-history of the author's group which saw itself as the 'remnant' of Israel spoken of by the prophets; in other words, the true Israel to which belongs the blessings of the future age. The Admonition accuses the *dorshe halakhot*, i.e. 'seekers of smooth things' who 'chose delusions and sought out loopholes ... and caused the covenant to be broken and the statute to be violated' (CD 1.18-20). This may be a subtle sarcasm against the Pharisees who derived *halakha* from Scripture in a more flexible manner than is found at Qumran. The second section, the 'Laws', is twice as long as the Admonition and sets forth regulations on various biblical topics, including priests, Gentiles, Sabbath, agricultural gifts, oaths, diet, ritual purity and marriage. The author's brand of exegesis is stringent throughout.

Unlike the Community Rule (1QS), which is an organizational document for the sect which lived at Qumran, the laws of the Damascus Document are considered by the author applicable to all Jews wherever they might live in the land of Israel. Marrying and raising families throughout the land of Israel, adherents maintained their own property and income (CD 14.12-13). The Qumran Community may be an offshoot of the group which produced the Damascus Document, perhaps a more rigorous subset which shunned marriage and family life for a certain period of time so that adherents could devote themselves to holier tasks (Talmon 1994: 8-9).

The emphasis on purity is clearly stated in the Damascus Document. One of the author's 'three nets of Belial', is the defilement of the Temple (CD 4.15-17). One reason for this defilement was the fact that some Jews were sleeping with menstruants (CD 5.7). The writer emphasizes the need to 'separate impure from pure and differentiate between holy and common' (CD 12.19-20). Those who entered the new covenant in the land of Damascus agreed to set apart holy portions according to the proper interpretation. According to the author, no impure person may bring an offering nor enter the house of prostration (CD 11.17-22).

Those who 'walk according to these matters in perfect holiness' are celibate, but others who 'reside in the camps in accordance with the rule of the land and take women and beget children' are married (CD 7.5-7). The higher level of purity excludes physically or mentally disabled persons and under-age boys from the camp since the 'holy angels are in its midst' (CD 15.1). In addition, the Damascus Document prohibits sexual intercourse in Jerusalem, the 'City of the Temple' (CD 12.1-2). In ordinary cities, sexual intercourse seems to be for procreation only. The text forbids '*zenut* with one's wife' which is somewhat unclear but probably refers to sexual intercourse for pleasure (4Q270 7 i 13; 4Q269, frag. 12), and marital relations were explicitly forbidden during pregnancy (4Q270; Baumgarten 1995a: 448).

Ritual impurity and transgression are linked. Anyone who sins must, in addition to repentance, undergo water purification. The text states, 'No one who has consciously transgressed anything of a precept is to be believed as a witness against his fellow, until he has been purified to return' (CD 10.2). Another connection between sin and impurity is the fact that exclusion from the 'purity' (= pure food) of the community is used as a penalty for wrongdoing. For example, the slanderer must keep away from the pure food for one year (4Q267 18.4; cf. 4Q265; 1QS 8.17-24). Sometimes just the accusation of a crime by a single witness is enough to exclude a person from the purity (CD 9.17-23). The accused is penalized by withholding of food but, more importantly, the community's food and personnel are protected from defilement by someone that is morally unreliable.

Some of the impurity bearers of Leviticus 12–15 are associated in the Damascus Document with moral failure. Several of the Cave 4 fragments consider leprosy, i.e. various skin diseases, a plague sent by God on sinners, a notion implicit already in the Bible (see Chapter 4). Some fragments attribute the disease to an evil spirit which enters the body and interferes with the flow of blood (4Q266 2–3; 4Q267 9.1; cf. t. *Neg.* 6.7; b. *Ber.* 5b). Also the *zab*, a man with an abnormal sexual flow, is considered a sinner by the Damascus Document (4Q266, 4Q272). By contrast, Rabbinic sages insist that if the condition resulted from sexual fantasies it was not considered the biblical disease (m. *Zab.* 2.2). Both lepers and gonorrheics are in a catalogue of transgressors in 4Q270 9 ii.

Menstrual impurity is rigidly defined in the Damascus Document. As noted, Jews are rebuked for having sexual intercourse with menstruants, thereby polluting the sanctuary (CD 5.7; cf. 4Q266 6 ii 2; cf. Lev. 15.24; Ezek. 18.6). The author considers any blood discharged outside of the seven-day menstrual period as abnormal and defines the woman as a *zabah*, a much more impure person (4Q266 6 ii 2-4). This contrasts with the more flexible Rabbinic law under which a woman is not a *zabah* unless she has had three consecutive days of bleeding outside of her normal period (*Sif. meṣ. zab. par.* 5.9).

The new mother conveys more impurity than a simple reading of Scripture requires. The Damascus Document mentions a wet nurse for the baby, evidently because the mother would convey impurity to her child through her milk (4Q266 6 ii 11; Baumgarten, 1996: 57). Also, like other Dead Sea Scrolls, the Damascus Document considers the foetus a separate life (4Q270 9 xi 15-17; Baumgarten 1995a: 445-48). Thus the author would probably agree with the Temple Scroll that if a foetus dies inside its mother, it is considered a corpse and so renders the mother impure as a grave (11Q19 50.10-19). Miqṣat Ma'aśe ha-Torah seems to reflect the same principle in its rule that an animal found alive inside the womb of a slaughtered animal requires separate slaughter.

Pure-food laws found in the Damascus Document derive from a strict interpretation of Scripture. The prohibited 'swarmers' of Leviticus 11 are interpreted to include even small organisms, such as bee larvae or any sea creature (CD 12.11-13). Even fish had to be ritually slaughtered and the blood drained (CD 12.13-14).

Also, like other Qumran scrolls, the Damascus Document regards the contagion of impurity in a maximal fashion. All wood, stones and dust within the house of the dead could transmit impurity if moistened with oil (CD 12.15-17). The author regards all *kelim* (items susceptible to impurity) within the house of the dead subject to impurity, including 'any vessel, nail, or peg in a wall' (CD 12.17-18; cf. Num 19.14-15). The Rabbis understand *kelim* to refer only to those items listed in Leviticus 11.32: earthenware, leather and fabric, and these must form usable utensils or vessels (m. *Kel.* 2.1; *Sif. Num.* 126[162]).

Some stringencies concern purification. Immersion pools had to be of requisite size, i.e. enough 'to cover a man', in order to be effective; one which was not large enough was defined as a 'vessel' (CD 10.11-13; cf. Lev. 15.16 which commands a man to wash 'all his body' after sexual intercourse). If the requisite amount is not there in the pool (to cover), that water will be contaminated by the impure person's touch (CD 10.13; cf. Leviticus 11.36ff where a fountain or pit 'wherein there is plenty of water' is immune to impurity). The Mishnah too makes a distinction between a vessel and a *miqveh*, and defines the size of the latter explicitly (m. *Miq.* 1). The Damascus Document does not consider impurity bearers pure until the sun has set on the day of their immersion (4Q266 9 ii 1-4). This contrasts with the Rabbinic allowance for the *tebul yom*, the one who has immersed but is still waiting for sunset, to function in every way as a pure individual except with regard to sancta (cf. m. *TY* 2.1; 3.6).

Since the priests are the custodians of the purity laws, it comes as no surprise that they are especially prominent in them. Only the priest, even if he is a simpleton, may pronounce leprosy (CD 13). Priests who have been captives among the Gentiles may not officiate or even approach sancta: 'He should not approach the service ... within the curtain and should not eat of the most holy things' (4Q266 5 ii 5-7; 4Q267, 6 ii 5-9; Baumgarten 1992a: 509 and private communication). Jews are admonished to provide the necessary offerings for the priests. At the other end of the spectrum, Gentiles are to be avoided. The Damascus Document restricts selling animals, produce and servants to Gentiles (CD 12.11). Any metals which Gentiles had used for idolatry were permanently forbidden for Jewish use (4Q269 8.1-3; *contra* m. *AZ* 3.2 where the

Rabbis allow the 'nullification' of idolatrous metals, especially if the images are broken, Baumgarten 1996: 131). Of course, those who disagreed with the author, even though they may have been Jewish, were considered false Israelites and as much outsiders as non-Jews.

As apparent from the above discussion, there are clear connections between the purity laws of the Damascus Document and those of other Qumran texts. Most notably, the 'camp' of 'holy perfection' described in the Damascus Document (CD 7.6-7) reminds one of the celibate community at Qumran. The 4Q manuscripts of the Damascus Document reveal a striking parallel to the penal code of the Community Rule in both substance and in wording (Baumgarten 2000: 168–69). The linkage of moral and ritual impurity, characteristic of many Qumran documents, is also present in the Damascus Document. The severe definition of a woman's menstrual discharge and the laws governing childbirth too reveal similarities with other Qumran texts. In contrast to the Mishnah, the interpretation of the Damascus Document is found to be more stringent in several instances.

3. Temple Scroll

The Temple Scroll is probably the oldest text discovered at Qumran. The original composition is believed to date back to the mid-second century BCE. Although there may be as many as five manuscripts extant, only two, dating to the Herodian period, are certain copies of this text: 11Q19 and 11Q20.

The author of the Temple Scroll rewrites large parts of the Pentateuch in first-person style, presenting his view of the laws as God's direct discourse to Israel. The main presentation has to do with the correct description of the Temple and its cult. F. García Martínez has identified four main themes: (1) construction of the Temple; (2) cycle of festivals (wheat, wine, oil, wood); (3) purity rules; (4) reworking of the laws of Deut. 12–23 (García Martínez 2000: 929).

Most scholars concur that the Temple Scroll is older than the formation of the sect at Qumran. There is no renewal of the covenant festival in the Temple Scroll, nor are organizational rules set out for the daily life of a community. Laws of idolatry, oaths and vows are not quite the same, neither is celibacy enjoined (Schiffman 1994b: 54). Furthermore, the vocabulary and presentation of the Temple Scroll are much different than in the other Qumran documents, and its views are presented not as exegesis but as direct revelation from Sinai.

The Temple Scroll reveals less antagonism toward its opponents on the subject of holiness than is found in other Qumran texts. As Jacob Milgrom says:

> [the Temple Scroll] does not betray any of the sectarianism prevalent in the other Qumran documents. The latter have withdrawn the attribute of holiness from all of Israel and have expropriated it as the exclusive property of the sect (*1QS* 1, 12-13; 2, 9. 16; 5, 13. 18; 8, 17. 21. 14; *CD* 4, 6; 8, 28; *1QM* 12, 1). Thus, whereas the Temple Scroll and *Jubilees* hope that their teachings will ultimately be accepted by all of Israel, the rest of Qumran has long despaired of this prospect; those outside its community are irretrievably doomed. (Milgrom 1993: 282, punctuation and italics as in original)

Polemics throughout the Scroll are muted.

Nevertheless, there is a large affinity between the Temple Scroll and other Qumran documents on particular purity matters (Milgrom 1990b: 95). Like the Damascus Document, the Temple Scroll prohibits sexual relations within the holy city (11Q19 45.11-12; CD 12.1-2; cf. 1QM 7.3 which excludes women from the holy camp). Like 4Q251, the author observes grain, wine and oil festivals (11Q19 43.3ff; 4Q251, frag. 9). Just as the Rule of the Congregation excludes the impure and the disabled from participation in the community, the Temple Scroll excludes them from the Temple City (11Q19 45.7-18; 1Q28a 2.5; cf. 1QM 7.4-6; MMT B 51–57). Names on the Temple's door match those on the gates of the New Jerusalem. Purification processes require a wait until sunset (11Q19 50.12-16; 51.2-5; cf. 4Q284a; 4Q266 9 ii 1-4; 4Q394 1. (16-20). Wood, stone and earth are susceptible to impurity (11Q19 49.12-16; cf. CD 12.15-17). Also the emphasis on Levites is found in other Qumran texts. Perhaps the Temple Scroll represents the priestly circles which spawned the emergent community before it moved to Qumran (García Martínez 2000: 931).

The purity source of the Temple Scroll (cols. 45-51) seems appropriate for the period of Antiochene crisis. Josephus discusses the holy status of Jerusalem during the time of Antiochus III and the desecration of the Temple by Antiochus IV. Purification was a major concern of the Maccabees. Josephus' claim that the major sects emerged at this time is entirely credible in light of the halakha presented in the Temple Scroll and other Qumran texts. Priests who disagreed with the way the cult was being conducted under the Hasmoneans dreamed of a future Temple where everything would be conducted in accordance with their view of God's law.

The fundamental principle underlying the purity laws of the Temple Scroll is that the sanctity of the Temple, resulting from God's presence in it, is so strong that it radiates outward to the entire city, requiring all persons who live or enter there to meet a high standard of purity. No sexual relations are allowed within the Temple city. The Torah's laws barring impure or disabled priests from officiating in the sanctuary are extended and applied to anyone entering the city. Special places were designated for the impure during their time of purification (at least three days) outside of the city. Similar places were established within ordinary cities, which also had to maintain a strict standard of purity, albeit not as intense as in the Temple city.

The purity laws of the Temple Scroll, like other Qumran documents, represent a maximalist interpretation of Scripture compared to the Rabbis of the Mishnah, who are minimalists. For instance, the Temple Scroll, like the Damascus Document, claims that everything in the house of the dead becomes impure (11Q19 49.11-16), whereas the Rabbis limit this contamination to only items the Bible specifically mentions as susceptible. Another example of such stringency is that, while both groups ostracize the leper from the community, the Temple Scroll banishes all impure persons from the community and establishes special places for them (11Q19 48.15-17).

Purification procedures reflect those in other Qumran scrolls. The author rejects the notion that a person can be considered pure before the end of the purification process (11Q19 50.12-16; cf. also 4Q266 9 ii 1-4; 4QMMT). However, like other Qumran texts, the Temple Scroll requires first-day ablutions for impurity bearers, apparently in order to allow them to eat their own food, though not the pure food of the community (11Q19 45.8-9; 4Q514 2; 4Q274; 4Q284).

The interlacing of moral and ritual purity is not apparent in the Temple Scroll (Klawans 2000: 48, 51). Purification does not appear to require atonement. The Temple Scroll generally reserves its purity language for the ritual impurities discussed in cols. 45-51.

4. 4QMiqṣat Ma'aśe ha-Torah (MMT)

Six manuscripts of Miqṣat Ma'aśe ha-Torah have been found at Qumran. The earliest of them date back to the second half of the first century BCE (Schiffman 2000b: 558). The text appears to be a letter written to the leaders of the religious establishment in Jerusalem. Some translate the title, 'Some Rulings Pertaining to the Torah', while others refer to it as the 'Halakhic Letter' or simply 'MMT'.

The laws of MMT revolve around two central topics: ritual purity and sacrifices. The authors list about twenty matters of Jewish law that, they insist, are being violated by the priests in authority, forcing a schism between them. It is interesting to note that this conflict did not arise from theological differences but from disagreement over the proper way to conduct the cult and maintain ritual purity. MMT reveals opposition to the existing priesthood under Hasmonean rule. The significance of MMT for our discussion lies primarily in its evidence of the seriousness with which many Jews of the Second Temple period took the issue of impurity. In the case of the sect, along with calendrical differences, it appears to be the fundamental reason for its split from the rest of Judaism. As E. Qimron and J. Strugnell, the earliest modern editors of MMT, put it, 'In early Judaism, contaminating the Temple was considered the most severe sin' (Qimron and Strugnell 1994: 132).

MMT's view of proper cultic procedures is usually quite stringent and the author accuses his opponents of laxity (cf. also the Psalms Pesher, *ki bahru bekalut*, 4Q171 1-2 i 19 and CD 1.18-20, which opposes 'seekers of smooth things'). Gentile offerings are apparently forbidden (MMT B 8–9; cf. m. *Zeb.* 4.5; *War* 2.409-10). Purity of any kind is not acknowledged until the end of the purification period. Curiously, some of MMT's laws match Rabbinic traditions about the Sadducees. For example, water flows contaminate both upward and downward. It may be that the early, pre-Hasmonean Sadducees were not compromising Hellenists but followed a very strict halakha (Schiffman 1990b: 435-57). In any case, MMT reflects the stance of an opposition party with a stringent approach to purity.

MMT reveals a strong relationship to other Dead Sea Scrolls, especially the Temple Scroll (Schiffman 1990b: 558). The calendar is the 364-day solar calendar used by the author of the Temple Scroll. MMT is in agreement with a variety of the Temple Scroll's sacrificial and purity laws, some of which may be polemics against the prevailing halakha, such as the rejection of the *tebul yom*, the impurity of skins of animals slaughtered outside of Jerusalem, rules regarding the slaughter of pregnant animals and other sacrificial laws, and the apportionment of fourth-year produce and animal tithes to priests. The entire city of Jerusalem is considered holy (MMT B 63). MMT shares purity concerns with other Scrolls as well. The author is concerned that the physically disabled and impure may defile sancta (MMT B 51–57; cf. 1Q28a 2.5; 11Q19 45.7-18; 1QM 7.4-6). The attitude of an opposition party with strong beliefs regarding purity is reflected as well in the Damascus Document (Schwartz 1996: 80). MMT does not detail rules for the organization of a sect and so has little in common with the Rule of the Community. Its terminology matches that found in other Qumran texts. Degrees of pure food are indicated by the terms *tohorah*, or ritually pure food of the sect, and *tohorat ha-miqdash*, sacred food. Many scholars concur that MMT derives from the formative period of the sect (García Martínez 1996: 27). Like the Temple

Scroll, MMT lacks the harsh language of sectarian antagonism; the tone is more conciliatory than later texts as the writer pleads with his addressees 'for your own benefit'.

5. Community Rule and Related Texts

The Community Rule is a foundation text for the Qumran sect which defines laws for the present, pre-messianic age. The text dates to the mid-second century BCE and several manuscripts of it have been found at Qumran (Cross 1994: 57). The Rule follows a solar calendar, as does *Jubilees*, Enoch and other texts, and the sect apparently prayed towards the sun in an effort to bring light to the earth. The text describes a celibate group following many stringent purity rules reserved in the Torah for the priesthood and holy warfare (Qimron and Charlesworth 1994: 3). This group shared all of their property in common (1QS 5.2ff) and subscribed to strict organizational rules, including procedures for new members, rules for administration, reproof, meetings and punishments. The ritual for the ceremony of entry and instructions for the annual renewal of the covenant are outlined in this text.

The Community Rule shows a striking relationship to the Damascus Document in terms of communal regulations. The common explanation is that the letter refers to Essenes living among all Israel while the Rule describes the organization of the wilderness group. While the precise relationship between the two documents is still debated, they emanate, at the very least, from related communities (Knibb 2000: 796).

Holiness and purity are key concerns of the Rule. The author refers to the sect as a 'house of holiness', a 'sanctuary in Aaron' and a 'house of truth in Israel'. Apparently, 4QS^{e} considers the community a sort of *miqdash* (sanctuary), as found in other Qumran texts (cf. 4Q174). While the laws of the Penal Code in the Rule do not dictate requirements of purity, the punishments do. Several penalties deprive the offender of the 'purity' (pure food) of the sect (1QS 7.1-27; 8.17-24; cf. 4Q267 18 iv; CD 9.17-23). This strong concern to maintain the purity of the community's food and members seems to reflect an effort to make up for the perceived corrupt and therefore defunct Jerusalem Temple. The Qumran sect conceived of its own community as a temporary substitute.

Candidates for admission to the sect are examined for purity (1QS 6.16-22). They are accepted in stages: (1) one year before they are allowed to eat pure food; and (2) two years before they are allowed pure drink. The author of 1QS, like the writer of 1QH, regards the human being as inherently impure, always requiring purification by the holy spirit as well as by ritual means (1QS 3.7-8; 11.9; 1QH 5[13].21; 9[1].22). Those who do not belong to the sect are hopelessly defiled.

5Q13, the Sectarian Rule, may be a version of 1QS or at least dependent on the same sources. Lawrence Schiffman suggests that the composition was as early as the second half of the second century BCE (Schiffman 1994a: 132). There is an overlap between the penal code of the two documents. The text discusses the ritual for the annual covenant renewal, prohibits non-members from the purification rituals of the sect, and includes a confession formula which must precede atonement and ritual purification.

5.1. Rule of the Congregation (1QSa=1Q28a) and Blessings (1QSb=1Q28b)

The Rule of the Congregation (or Messianic Rule) was written as an appendix copied on the same scroll as the Rule of the Community and followed by the Blessings (1Q28b). The original composition dates back to 100–75 BCE (Schiffman 2000c: 797). The text describes the eschatological community after the great war in terms of Zadokite leadership, normal family life, and a renewed emphasis on the Levites. It shows affinity with other Qumran texts, in particular the War Scroll, where the laws of the messianic congregation (1Q28a) and the military (1QM) are similar.

Like the War Scroll, the Rule of the Congregation excludes persons with ritual impurities and physical deformities, due to the presence of angels within the community (1Q28a 2.5; 11.3-11; 1QM 7.4-6). The Rule states that 'no one afflicted in body, crippled in legs or hands, lame, deaf, blind or dumb, or visibly blemished, or tottering may stand in the congregation due to the presence of the angels' (1Q28a 2.5). This emphasis on priestly standards is characteristic of Qumran texts. In the messianic procession, a priest will enter at the head of the Congregation of Israel and the other priests will sit with him.

Blessings (1Q28b), which follows the Rule of the Congregation, is also intended for the messianic age. God will restore the Sons of Zadok to their priestly functions in the eschaton (1Q28b 3.26). Significant for our topic of purity is the following blessing on the community, '[... May you] dedicate yourself for the Holy of Holies, for [... you are made] holy for him, and shall glorify his name and his holiness' (1Q28b 4.28). In this benediction, a sort of community mission statement becomes apparent: the sect's very purpose is to maintain holiness at a level which will bring glory to God (cf. 1QS 5.6; 8.5-6; 9.6).

5.2. War Scroll (1QM)

This Cave 1 document probably dates back to the late first century BCE or early first century CE (Davies 2000: 967). It describes an eschatological war between the sect, 'the Sons of Light', and its enemies, 'the Sons of Darkness'. The sect claims victory with the aid of heavenly forces. The text is ideologically connected with the Community Rule; both assume a certain dualism (1QM 13.1-6; 1QS 2.1-18). The organizational laws for the messianic community remind the reader of the Rule of the Congregation.

The presence of heavenly beings, or angels, within the camp makes a high standard of purity of utmost importance. Those who are impure or physically disabled are considered a threat to the continued holiness of the group; women too are excluded (1QM 7.4-6).

5.3. *1QPesher Habakkuk* (1QHabPesher)

The original text behind this Cave 1 document from the Herodian period is dated either to the second century BCE or to the first half of the first century BCE. There are two major subject areas: (1) internal religious politics of Jerusalem and its priesthood; and (2) the impending threat of the Kittim (probably the Romans). The text refers to the Wicked Priest, who was originally in line with the teaching of the sect but who then strayed and began to persecute the Teacher of Righteousness.

Purity language, e.g. *niddat tum'ah,* is used in the text but its meaning is vague. The author's accusation that the sanctuary is defiled may indicate lack of proper ritual procedures. However, he does not specify any cultic or purity infractions but focuses rather on transgressions of the moral sort. He points to several specific sins of the Wicked Priest, including arrogance, greed and theft. Like the biblical prophets, the author may simply be using the language of ritual impurity to describe the repulsiveness of sin.

5.4. 1QH Thanksgiving Scroll

This text is a poetic composition consisting of hymns of thanks to God. Manuscripts have been found in both Cave 1 and Cave 4, the earliest of which dates back to shortly after 100 BCE. The original text of 1QH, however, dates to the time of the Teacher of Righteousness in the second century BCE and so is considered one of the foundation documents of the Qumran Community. The hymns describe the suffering that the righteous endure and the vindication that will ultimately be the reward of the faithful.

Purity is a prerequisite for holiness: 'For your [God's] glory, you have purified man from sin, so that he can make himself holy for you from every impure abomination and blameworthy iniquity' (1QH 19[11].10-11). As in the War Scroll and the Rule of the Congregation, purification enables the righteous to 'take his place with the host of the holy ones ... with the congregation of the sons of heaven' (1QH 11[3].21-22; 1Q28a 2.5; 11.3-11; 1QM 7.6). As in the Community Rule, purification comes not by ablutions alone but also by repentance and divine forgiveness (1QH 11[3].21; 1QS 3.7-8).

The author considers himself a sinner in continuous need of God's grace for purification. He describes the human being as hopelessly depraved and inherently impure, 'foundation of shame, source of impurity, oven of iniquity, building of sin' (1QH 9 [1].22; cf. 22 [12].25), and 'He is a structure of dust shaped with water, his base is the guilt of sin, vile unseemliness, source of impurity, over which a spirit of degeneracy rules' (5[13]. 21; cf. 1QS 11.9). Thus, this text does not present impurity in terms of specific causes, effects and purification rituals, but as an ontological category resulting from the human condition.

6. 4QTohorot

Several Cave 4 fragments, numbering between 4Q274–78, are sometimes given the common rubric, Tohorot, or 'Purities', since they all deal with some aspect of ritual purity. They have also been termed with alphabetic sigla, e.g. Tohorot A [= 4Q274]; Tohorot B [= 4Q276–77]. All of these texts interpret biblical laws of ritual purification and contamination. Sectarian antagonism is not evident within them and some of the laws concern purity issues relating to women. Thus, they may date back to the second century BCE, before the sect's formal withdrawal to Qumran.

The typical Qumran notion of 'the purity' is implied in the Tohorot texts. In their effort to require maximum purity, it seems that these authors combined the purification rules addressed to all Israel in Leviticus 11–15 with the purity required to eat sacrificial portions in Leviticus 7.19-21. As a result of this 'homogenization', came the requirement that all Israelites bathe before eating any food. The Pharisees too bathed before eating, although probably not those who were isolated with extended, severe impurities (Lk. 11.38; Harrington 1995: 42–54).

The potency of liquids as conveyors of impurity is treated in fragment 3 of 4Q274. According to this text, crops which have become wet in any way, even by rain, become susceptible to impurity and all those who harvest them must be in a state of ritual purity. Agricultural laws played an important role in the community because food for the communal meals had to be pure from the time of harvesting to the point of consumption.

A similar concern over the purity of liquids is attested in other documents from Qumran. As we have seen already in the Damascus Document, oil stains in the house of the dead had to be removed so that corpse impurity would not spread (CD 12.15-17). The Temple Scroll insists that all liquid, even water stains, in such a house becomes impure and must be removed (11Q19 49.8-11). It is well known that access to communal drinks was granted to the novitiate at Qumran only after two to three years of probation (1QS 6.20; 7.20; cf. *War* 2.123).

This extra emphasis on liquids is brought into relief when compared with the Rabbinic system, where liquids were conveyors of impurity par excellence, yet rules concerning them were still not as stringent as among the sectarians. The Rabbis insisted that there must be *intentional* putting of water on the seed by permission of the owner in order for it to become susceptible to impurity (m. *Makh.* 1.1; 3.6; 5.11; 6.8; b. *Qid.* 59b). The issue of purity of the harvest was important to the Sages too, to the point that they quarantined the workers of the olive presses while they pressed the oil (m. *Toh.* 9–10). However, it was only at this stage, when liquid was pressed from the fruit, that impurity was allowed to become an issue.

Another principle which comes into relief in these texts is the difference in status between an ordinary person and one who has decided to live at a higher standard of purity (cf. the distinction between camps in the Damascus Document). Like the Temple Scroll, 4Q274 suggests that a purer person will not eat the contents of even a sealed vessel in the house of the dead (4Q274 3 ii; 11Q19 49.8; Baumgarten 1994a: 98). Scripture is clear that open vessels in such a house draw in impurity and so contaminate their contents (Num. 19.15). The implication, at least from a Rabbinic point of view, is that if the vessels had been sealed, they would have protected their contents from impurity.

Tohorot texts 4Q276–77 discuss the rite of the red cow, which was burned to produce ashes for purification from corpse contamination (Num 19.17-21). The Qumran text authenticates the ritual for the period of the Second Temple, for which the only evidence had heretofore been late Rabbinic texts (200 CE at the earliest).

The Pharisees and Sadducees of the Mishnah argued over the correct standard of purity for those who participated in the red cow rite. 4Q277 (1 ii 2) agrees with the Sadducean view which would not allow a person whose purification was still in process to participate in the ritual. The Pharisees, who ascribed to the *tebul yom* concept discussed above, would intentionally make the participants impure so that they would immerse, and, to the dismay of the Sadducees, be in this intermediate status when they performed the rituals (m. *Par.* 3.7). This insistence on full purification before participating in community activities surfaces in several Qumran texts (cf. 4Q266 9 ii 1-4; 4Q394 3-7 1. (16-20); 11Q19 51.2-5). Another sign of the priestly attitude typical of Qumran texts, Tohorot allows only a mature priest to sprinkle purgation water over the corpse-impure (4Q277 1 ii 6-7; cf. m. *Par.* 3.4 which implies that only young boys were allowed to sprinkle the purgation water, perhaps because of their lack of experience with sexual impurity, Baumgarten 1995b: 112–19).

One of the most significant assumptions in the Tohorot texts is that even impure persons, who continue in their impurity or purification for an extended period, must immerse themselves in water if they contract any further impurity (4Q274 1 i 3, 5, 9; Baumgarten 1994b: 273–78; Milgrom 1994b: 59–68). They would, of course, still be barred from the communal meal and have to eat separately but they would not have been allowed to eat at all unless they had bathed (cf. 4Q514; Milgrom 1994a: 177). Impure persons can become more impure.

Purifying persons pose a particular threat in terms of contaminating food because they are not sequestered away from the community, like impure persons, but must come within the camp in order to undergo purification. They must avoid susceptible, pure people and items because otherwise they will contaminate them.

Tohorot requires purification before the Sabbath and the festivals, i.e. purification should not take place on the holy day itself. A problem arises when, for example, a corpse-impure person is in the middle of the purification week when the Sabbath approaches, and requires sprinkling procedures during sacred time (4Q274 2 i). The text rules that such an individual must (1) make sure not to touch purities during the Sabbath and (2) wait until the Sabbath is over for the sprinkling procedure. The Mishnah too restricts purificational sprinkling on the Sabbath (m. *Pes.* 6.1-2).

Tohorot places the defilement of semen on a par with the flux of the *zab*, whose bed or chair defiles even without direct contact (Lev. 15). Those who handle anything which has been in contact with semen either directly or indirectly, for example by carrying a contaminated garment or mattress, become impure and must launder their clothes (4Q274 2 i 8). This is commensurate with the added stringency regarding semen reflected in the Temple Scroll, where entrance to the Temple City is denied for three days to those who have had a seminal emission (11Q19 45 11-12). For the Rabbis, semen does not have the potency to defile people without direct contact (b. *Naz.* 66a; m. *Zab.* 5.11; *Sif. meṣ. zab.* 2.8).

The close relationship between sin and impurity, often considered a hallmark of the Qumran sect, is found also in Tohorot. The first line of 4Q274 seems to restrict prayer during times of impurity: '[Let him not] begin to cast his sup[plica]tion. In a bed of sor[ro]w shall he li[e and in a] seat of sighing shall he sit.' This attitude coheres with other Qumran texts where a prayer for atonement is offered only after ritual purification (4Q512 10-11 x 2-5; 4Q414; 4Q284; cf. Sib. Or. 4.165-68; Life of Adam and Eve 6–7; Baumgarten 1999b: 102). This stands in contrast to the lack of plea in the prescribed Rabbinic blessing (b. *Ber.* 51a; b. *Pes.* 7b).

7. Other Cave 4 Texts

7.1. 4QFlorilegium (4Q174)

The extant manuscripts of 4QFlorilegium, consisting of 26 fragments, are dated to the second half of the first century BCE (Brooke 2000: 297). The text interprets various passages of Scripture and refers several times to the 'last days'. Of particular interest is the reference to the 'place' of 2 Sam. 7.10, which the author interprets as the eschatological Temple. In anticipation of this Temple, the author conceives of the sect itself as a sort of interim human sanctuary, *miqdash 'adam* (4Q174 1.6; Dimant 1986: 188). The 'works of thanksgiving', *ma'ase todah*, of these holy men function like sacrificial offerings.

7.2. 4Q249 Midrash Sefer Moshe 4Qpap cryptA

This text consists of 14 fragments of papyrus placed together according to their fibre patterns. The editor claims that Midrash Sefer Moshe is the text (or part of it) that the sect studied every night, the Midrash ha-Torah of 1QS 8.15 (Pfann 1999: 2). This would be surprising given the fact that the main subject seems to be the impurity of leprosy.

The extant document is primarily concerned with 'leprous houses'. Stones within a house which begin to exhibit the greenish or reddish tones of mildew must not only be scraped and removed from the house (Lev. 14) but must also be placed outside the city. If this hue returns to the house, it must be torn down.

The text uses the concrete case of mildew in a house to symbolize deceit within the king's house. Like leprosy, deceit spreads beyond its original location to affect neighbouring items/persons and must be uprooted entirely or its curse will affect everyone. The association of leprosy and sin has its roots in Scripture (cf. Lev. 14.34; Num. 12) and is assumed by other Qumran writers and Rabbinic interpretation as well (cf. 4Q512; 4Q274 frag. 1; see Chapter 4, 'Leprosy', below).

7.3. 4QHalakha A 4Q251

4QHalakha A, a fragment dating from the early Herodian period, discusses various aspects of biblical law. Typical Pentateuchal laws included are: penalties for the owner of a goring ox, Sabbath laws, required priestly contributions, and various incest regulations. Purity laws are prominent in this text.

Most of the purity laws of 4Q251 attempt to settle Scripture's ambiguity with regard to pure animals and food, purity concerns on which the Bible is either ambiguous or silent. According to 4Q251, the firstborn of all impure animals must be redeemed and given to the priests (4Q251 10.4-9). The Rabbis, noting that Scripture mentions only the redemption of firstborn donkeys, consider only this species affected (*Sif. Num.* 126). However, the Qumran author regards the donkey as simply representative of all unclean animals. Also, the Torah's various rules regarding pure-food laws are harmonized on the side of stringency. For example, Deuteronomy forbids eating *tref* (an animal which has become prey) (Deut. 14.20-21); Leviticus (Lev. 17.15) states that it incurs a one-day impurity but mentions no penalty. Exodus rejects *tref* but not *nebelah* (an animal which has died a natural death) (Exod. 22.30). 4Q251 combines these and forbids eating either (4Q251 12.3-4; cf. b. *Men.* 45a).

4Q251 is concerned with the sanctity of firstfruit offerings. Fragment 9 insists that no one eat grain, wine or oil until the firstfruits' day has come and they are given to the priests. Several other ancient sources ascribe to a pentecontad calendar where Jews offered firstfruits for barley, wheat, wine and oil at the times of their particular harvests (Baumgarten 1976: 36–46; Yadin 1983: 119–22). The Temple Scroll, in particular, explains that certain sacrifices and firstfruits are offered for each festival which desanctify or release the rest of the crop (11Q19 43.3ff). The Rabbis do not extend the firstfruit grain festivals to wine, oil or any other fruit.

4QHalakha A regulates the disposition of holy food. Fragment 15 refers to 'most holy dedications'. These cannot be eaten by a priest's household, only by the priest himself. The priest's household may eat of his other food gifts (frag. 16). However, a *zonah* (woman who has had forbidden sexual relations) and a *ḥallalah* (daughter of a priest and a prohibited woman), even if married to a priest, cannot eat his food. Also the fruit of trees in their fourth year is given to the priests since it is holy to God (Lev. 19.23-24). This notion is emphasized in other Qumran texts (11Q19 60.2-4; 4QMMT B 62–63; 4Q266 6 iv; 4Q270) but was opposed by the later Rabbis, who allowed fourth-year fruit to be eaten by its owners as long as they brought it up to Jerusalem.

7.4. 4QMiscellaneous Rules 4Q265 [or 4QSerekh Damascus 4QSD]

4Q265 consists of seven identified and several unidentified fragments. The contents are diverse, ranging from penal code violations and Sabbath rules to a discussion of Adam and Eve in Paradise.

The version of the penal code found in fragment 4 is interesting from the standpoint of purity. First, moral and social violations are punished by exclusion from the purity (food), a notion found in other Scrolls (1QS 8.17-24; 4Q267 18, 4; CD 9.17-23). Secondly, new candidates to the 'council of the community' are instructed for one year and then examined; however, they are not admitted to the liquids of the community for another year. This procedure is known already from the Community Rule (1QS 6.16-22; 7.20).

Like other Qumran texts, 4Q265 emphasizes the need for purity on the Sabbath and other holy days (cf. 4Q251; 4Q274 2 i). Soiled *(so'im)* garments are forbidden on the Sabbath (4Q265 6.2). Nevertheless, the act of purification must not be performed on the holy day itself. Priests may not sprinkle purification water on the Sabbath, and they are not even allowed to bathe or launder clothes on Yom Kippur (4Q265 7.3-4; cf. also 4Q274 1 ii; 4Q251 1; cf. m. *Pes.* 6.2).

Fragment 7 includes a discussion of the Garden of Eden which can only be understood in light of purity laws. Joseph Baumgarten explains that the Garden of Eden is a prototype of the Temple. Using the book of *Jubilees*, Baumgarten restores blanks in lines 11-13. Adam does not come to the Garden immediately and neither does Eve. They probably wait 40 and 80 days, respectively, taking into account the impurity of childbirth (Lev. 12.4-5), like the *Jubilees* version. The new couple does not partake of any fruit of the Garden until after this period, since all of the Garden's contents is considered holy (Cf. *Jub.* 3.12; 1QH^{a} 16.10-13). This text seems to indicate that the newborn child (as well as its mother) is impure until the 40/80 days are completed. Similarly, the Damascus Document suggests that the child will become impure through nursing, which it forbids during the mother's impurity (4Q266 6 ii 11). Scripture explicitly refers only to the mother's impurity (Lev. 12.4-5; but cf. Lk. 2.22). A theological principle found in other Qumran texts may be surfacing here as well: humanity is born in an impure condition, coming into the world brings impurity (even for Adam and Eve) (cf. 1QH 9.22; 1QS 9.9-10).

Another interesting issue in 4Q265 concerns the purity of women. According to fragment 3 no woman nor young man is allowed to eat of the Passover sacrifice (cf. also 11Q19 17.8-9). Joseph Baumgarten states that while this notion is found also in *Jubilees* (*Jub.* 49.17) and the Temple Scroll (11Q19 17.8-9), both of which require males 20 years old and upwards to eat the Passover in the Temple courts, it is not in the writings of Josephus or the Rabbis (*War* 6.426; m. *Pes.* 8.1). Baumgarten concludes that the Qumran author is concerned that men sharing their Passover portions with their families may compromise the purity of the meal, since the rest of the family might not be pure (Baumgarten 1999b: 64).

7.5. 4QPurification Liturgy 4Q284 [or Laws for Purification]

Several fragments make up the existing text of 4Q284. Fragment 1 begins in the middle of a discussion of the festal calendar. The text then mentions 'purgation water', *me niddah*, and in the next line, 'semen'. A possible interpretation is that at festivals the sect required purification with *me niddah* to neutralize any possible corpse or carcass impurity a person may have contracted, knowingly or not. Alternatively, the group may have used the stronger purification of *me niddah* for purification from all impurities (Baumgarten 1999b: 83–87).

Fragments 2–3 discuss a person undergoing a week-long purification, probably the corpse-impure person. Several points are clear: (1) he shall not eat before purification; (2) his touch causes impurity; (3) sprinkling water is used; (4) in order to complete the full seven-day purification the purifying person must wait for sunset on the seventh day; and (5) a blessing marks the end of the purification period.

This text is similar to others found at Qumran, these fragments affirming polemics apparent in other Qumran texts. First, purification does not occur before sunset. Secondly, a reference to 'true purity' may be a hint that other systems of purity were not considered authentic. Finally, it is helpful to read 4Q284 in light of 4Q514, where the purifying person, although not completely pure, may eat after bathing on the days of his purifying process. Otherwise, one wonders how the purifying person is expected to survive during an extended (more than one day) time of impurity. Other fragments of 4Q284 are not substantial.

7.6. 4Q Harvesting 4Q284a [or Laws about Gleaning]

This Cave 4 text is in two fragments. Fragment 1 describes the harvesting of figs, pomegranates and olives. The whole process of harvesting must be done in purity. Impure persons and those who are not full members of the sect may not harvest produce. If they do, they will contaminate the fruit via its juice. Fruit must be squeezed and eaten in purity. Fragment 2 adds a mention of dew, probably to indicate that the moisture of dew is sufficient to render a crop susceptible to impurity. This is contrary to the Rabbinic system in which rain and dew do not make a crop susceptible to impurity since they are completely outside of a farmer's control. Fragment 2 also states that the men of the community will do the harvesting.

This text shares the concerns of Tohorot regarding not only eating fruit in purity but also harvesting and pressing it in purity. Apparently, non-members are considered contaminating to the fruit just as impure persons are. Food of any kind must be free from impurity, not just the priestly portions but every food item that appears on the communal table. This reminds one of the *Ḫaberim*, who ate all food in purity.

7.7. Ritual of Purification A 4Q414

The Ritual of Purification A records the rituals and blessing of the purification process. The text refers to 'those purified for his fixed times [festivals]'. Like 4QPurification Liturgy, the writer emphasizes the importance of the festivals from the standpoint of purity as times of special inspection for impurity, both moral and ritual.

4Q512 is very similar to 4Q414. Both documents deal with ablutions, purification blessings, leprosy and corpse contamination. Like 4Q512, 4Q414 reveals the number of blessings, both before and after purification, which the purifying person was obliged to offer. The procedure, based on similarities with 4Q414 69 ii 7, is outlined by Esther Eshel as follows: (1) prayer before immersion; (2) immersion and sprinkling; and (3) two blessings (Eshel 1999: 147).

The initial bathing of the purifying person, found in other Qumran texts, is also championed by 4Q414 (4Q284; 4Q274; 4Q514; cf. also Tob. 2.9). Fragment 2 mentions a first-, third- and seventh-day purification for corpse impurity as referenced in the Temple Scroll (11Q19 45.8-9); Scripture only requires third- and seventh-day purifications (Num. 19). Curiously, *miqva'ot* have been found at cemeteries: (1) tombs of Helena of Adiabene and (2) in the courtyard of a burial cave at Jericho (Eshel 1999: 139).

The language of atonement is used in the context of ritual purification as seen elsewhere at Qumran (1QS; 4Q512). Here the divine *ḥoq kippur*, 'law of atonement', is paralleled with *tohorat ṣedeq*, the state of 'righteous purity' (4Q414 13 i 2-4). The purifying person blesses God for his willingness to grant him atonement. He knows that ritual purification alone cannot effect purity if one falls short of God's approval. It is not that he cannot distinguish between ritual impurity and sin, it is just that this distinction in the larger picture carries little meaning. Impurity of any kind will prevent access to God.

7.8. 4QHalakha C 4Q472a

4QHalakha C is a fragment from the early Herodian period with only about ten complete words legible. The key words for our purposes are *mikhse ṣo*. Joseph Baumgarten understands *ṣo* to be an abbreviated form of *so'ah*, and reads 'covering excrement'. Josephus refers to a section along Jerusalem's western wall as *Bethso*, a term which probably means *Beit So'ah*, latrine (Yadin 1983: 303), and explains that Essenes used a hatchet to dig a hole for defecation and burial of their excrement so as not to offend the 'divine rays of light' (*War* 2.148). *Shalish*, another clear word in 4QHalakha C, can be translated 'hollowed hatchet' and may refer to the practice described by Josephus (cf. Isa. 40.12; Baumgarten cited in Elgvin 1999: 156). This text is significant in that it supports the identification of the sect with Josephus' Essenes.

Other Qumran texts stand with 4QHalakha C that excrement is a cause of ritual impurity. 4Q265 prohibits use of garments soiled with excrement on the Sabbath (4Q265 6.2). The Temple Scroll rules that latrines had to be built 3000 cubits away from the sanctuary (11Q19 46.15; 4Q265 7 i 3) and at the same time forbids walking more than 2000 cubits on the Sabbath. The feasibility of such laws aside, it is apparent that the sect regarded the impurity of excrement as a serious matter. This contrasts sharply with the view of the Mishnah that excrement does not cause ritual impurity.

7.9. 4QRitual of Purification B 4Q512

Several fragments consisting of blessings by the purifying person make up the text known as 4Q512. Various impurities are discussed. Column 3 mentions '*kol 'ervat basarenu*' which probably refers to human impurity in general, as in column 5 where the purifier asks for grace for all hidden acts of guilt. The purifications apparently take place before festivals. In column 8 the impure person thanks God for [delivering] him from *pesha*ʿ, 'sin', and for purifying him from ʿ*ervat niddah*. Also in column 8, the leper explicitly confesses 'I have sinned'. Column 10 describes a *zab*'s purification blessing; he prays *after* he puts his clothes on. Column 12 discusses purification from a corpse. The purifier thanks God for *kippur*, atonement from guilt. Also, several columns give thanks to God for purification and for creating a holy people.

The mixture of ritual and moral purity distinctive of the Qumran texts is understandable. The idea is that both moral atonement and ritual purity are required to receive God's grace. Impurity of any kind will separate a person from the community and from God's presence. All impurity was in some way tainted and required penitence and perhaps *me niddah*. The sect was reading the biblical text too carefully not to notice the distinctions present for different types of impurity. However, these distinctions are of lesser importance than the underlying principle that impurity of any kind separates a person from God.

7.10. 4QOrdinances B 4Q513

4Q513, or Ordinances B, interprets various biblical laws according to a different system than that found in the Mishnah. The text extant is not later than the first century BCE (Schiffman 1994a: 146). In Qumran style, interpretations are strict, including prohibitions regarding the *ʿomer* and blowing the shofar on the Sabbath outside of Temple precincts.

In the matter of purity, concern for the purity of priests and holy food is at a premium. The writer emphasizes that the daughters of priests are not to marry non-Jews (cf. 4QMMT B 75–82). If they were to intermarry, neither these women nor their families would be allowed to eat of priestly contributions or even to touch any pure food (cf. 4Q251 frags. 15-16). There are other purity laws in the text, including the concern of oil transmitting impurity (cf. CD 12.16; 11Q19 49.8-11), the prohibition on using an immersion pool which is too shallow (cf. CD 10.11-13), and some laws too fragmentary to decipher.

The characteristic Qumran blend of ritual and moral impurity is evident in 4Q513 as well. According to Ordinances B, the mixture of ordinary food with priestly food results in *ʿavon zimmah*, the 'sin of immorality' (4Q513 11.3).

7.11. 4QPurification Rule 4Q514 [4QOrdinances C]

The Purification Rule states that an impure person is forbidden to eat any food until undergoing an initial purification. At first this seems to be contrary to other Qumran texts which emphasize the impurity of a purifying individual until sunset of the final purificatory day. However, as Jacob Milgrom has explained, the Rule is in accord with other Qumran texts (Milgrom 1994a: 177–79). Impure persons may not eat of the communal *tohorah* until they are completely purified but they may eat their own food after ablutions (i.e. bathing and laundering) on the first day. This notion is familiar from other Qumran texts (4Q414 frag. 2; 4Q274; 4Q284).

Further Reading

Baumgarten, J.M.

1996 *Qumran Cave Four XIII: The Damascus Document (4Q266–273), Discoveries in the Judaean Desert XVIII* (Oxford: Clarendon Press).

1999a 'The Purification Liturgies', in *The Dead Sea Scrolls after Fifty Years*, II, eds. P. Flint and J.C. VanderKam (Leiden: E.J. Brill): 202–12.

1999b *Qumran Cave 4 XXV: Halakhic Texts, Discoveries in the Judaean Desert XXXV* (Oxford: Clarendon Press).

2000 'Damascus Document', *Encyclopedia of the Dead Sea Scrolls*, I, eds. L.H. Schiffman and J.C. VanderKam (New York: Oxford University Press): 166–70.

Bernstein, M. and J. Kampen (eds.)
1996 *Reading MMT: New Perspectives on Qumran Law and History* (Atlanta: Scholars Press).

Brooke, G.
2000 'Florilegium', in *Encyclopedia of the Dead Sea Scrolls*, I, eds. L.H. Schiffman and J.C. VanderKam (New York: Oxford University Press): 297–98.

Cross, F.
1994 'Appendix: Paleographical Dates of the Manuscripts', in *The Dead Sea Scrolls: Hebrew, Aramaic, and Greek Texts with English Translations. Vol. 1: Rule of the Community and Related Documents*, ed. J.H. Charlesworth (Tübingen: J.C.B. Mohr [Paul Siebeck]; Louisville, KY: Westminster/ John Knox Press): 57.

Knibb, M.
2000 'Rule of the Community' in *Encyclopedia of the Dead Sea Scrolls*, II, eds. L.H. Schiffman and J.C. VanderKam (New York: Oxford University Press): 793–97.

Licht, J.
1965a *Megillat Ha-Serakhim* (Jerusalem: Bialik Institute).

Qimron, E. and J.H. Charlesworth
1994 'Rule of the Community', in *The Dead Sea Scrolls: Hebrew, Aramaic, and Greek Texts with English Translations. Vol. 1: Rule of the Community and Related Documents*, ed. J.H. Charlesworth (Tübingen: J.C.B. Mohr [Paul Siebeck]; Louisville, KY: Westminster/John Knox Press): 1–5.

Qimron, E. and J. Strugnell
1994 *Qumran Cave 4 V: Miqṣat Ma'ase ha-Torah*, DJD X (Oxford: Clarendon Press).

Schiffman, L.H.
1990b '*Miqṣat Ma'aseh ha-Torah* and the Temple Scroll', *RevQ* 14: 435–57.
1994a 'Ordinances and Rules' and 'Sectarian Rule 5Q13', in *The Dead Sea Scrolls: Hebrew, Aramaic, and Greek Texts with English Translations. Vol. 1: Rule of the Community and Related Documents*, ed. J.H. Charlesworth (Tübingen: J.C.B. Mohr [Paul Siebeck]; Louisville, KY: Westminster/ John Knox Press): 132–75.
1996 'The Place of 4QMMT in the Corpus of Qumran Manuscripts', in *Reading MMT: New Perspectives on Qumran Law and History*, eds. M. Bernstein and J. Kampen, (Atlanta: Scholars Press): 81–98.
2000b 'Miqtsat Ma'asei ha-Torah', in *Encyclopedia of the Dead Sea Scrolls*, I, eds. L.H. Schiffman and J.C. VanderKam (New York: Oxford University Press): 558–60.
2000c 'Rule of the Congregation', in *Encyclopedia of the Dead Sea Scrolls*, II, eds. L.H. Schiffman and J.C. VanderKam (New York: Oxford University Press): 797–99.

Yadin, Y.
1983 *The Temple Scroll*, I-III (Jerusalem: The Exploration Society).

PART II

THE IMPURITIES

3

CORPSE IMPURITY

1. Introduction

Throughout the Graeco-Roman world there were taboos with regard to the impurity of the dead. In accordance with Greek tradition, water vessels stood outside the home of the deceased to mark it as impure and to provide purification for those visiting the bereaved. At Iulis and Athens the house of the dead person was sprinkled with sea water for purification. Romans considered corpse impurity potent enough to travel along family lines to relatives, even if they were not present at the funeral.

Corpse impurity was an especially serious matter if it came into contact with the sacred. According to the laws of Solon, anyone who came into contact with a corpse was banned from sacred precincts and worship of the gods. Priests at Coan were not allowed to enter the house of death for five days after the deceased was removed (Parker 1983: 38, 52). Peristratus demanded that the dead be removed from the Island of Delos if their graves were even within sight of the sanctuary. It is said that a plague afflicted the Delians since they had allowed burial on the sacred island. The goddess Artemis was not allowed even to look at death and thus had to abandon the mortal Hippolytus, for whom death was inescapable. If a shrine was ever polluted by the impurity of death, its efficacy was immediately neutralized. In the Antigone, birds of prey carrying scraps of a corpse to an altar consequently interrupted the contact between god and man (Parker 1983: 33).

The corpse is the most contaminating of all the impurity bearers in the Hebrew Bible (see Chapter 1, Table 1). Those who became impure, by contact with the dead or simply by entering a house where the dead lay, had to undergo a week of purification before they could return to community life. If they refused, they were to be ostracized from Israel (Lev. 7.21; 15.31; Num. 19.13, 20). The corpse-contaminated person was forbidden to approach sancta and so could not offer anything at the Temple (Lev. 7.19-20; Num. 9.7-11; Deut. 26.14; cf. m. *Kel.* 1.8). A person who was impure at the time of Passover was required to wait and celebrate the feast one month later (Num. 9.7-11; 2 Chron. 30.3).

In the Second Temple period corpse impurity became a more pressing issue among Jews. This was due in part to the desire of many Jews to replicate the purity of the sanctuary, as much as possible, in their own homes. The Pharisees, for example, applied priestly standards to their own food when they forbade any impure person to eat with them. Likewise, the Qumran sect barred the corpse-impure from the communal meal.

Burial was a primary concern at Qumran. The Temple Scroll, reiterating the Torah, insists that corpses must be buried on the same day that the person expires, otherwise the land becomes defiled (11Q19 64.2; cf. 1 Sam. 31.11-13). At Qumran, the dead were separated in a cemetery four metres away from the east wall of the complex. This burial ground contains about 1200 graves, all of which are oriented north to south. The graves are not family tombs; each of those excavated contained an individual male corpse. The 16 women and children discovered at the site were buried separately in extensions of the main cemetery, and in the south cemetery, and may even be of recent origin (Zias: 1999).

This chapter examines the impurity of the dead in three categories: (1) contamination; (2) purification; and (3) significance. The Qumran laws regarding the corpse are derived from the Torah but represent a very stringent interpretation. Some of this stringency is apparent in actual practice at Qumran while much of it is an ideal of what would be practised in Jerusalem if the sectarians had control of the cult. As we analyse the available data from Qumran, we will refer to Rabbinic practice, which reveals a high correspondence to the Qumran data and which often clarifies the fragmentary data at hand and the issues involved.

2. Contamination

Corpse impurity is the most potent of any ritual impurity discussed in the Bible, at Qumran or in Rabbinic literature. According to the Rabbis, it is an invisible substance which fills containers and escapes through holes and entrances (m. *Oh.* 13.1, 4; 15.8; t. *Oh.* 14.4). J. Neusner's description is apt: 'a kind of invisible, dense, and heavy gaseous substance, which will flow out of the specified substances if not contained by a barrier of some sort, but which, if contained by a wall, will then not evaporate upward' (Neusner 1976: 47). The one exception to this general rule is a grave. Corpse impurity is believed to spurt upwards through a grave contaminating anyone who walks over it. This description is also appropriate among the Qumran sect. Corpse impurity was a contagious force analogous to an invisible gas.

The contamination power of a corpse can be discussed in three categories: the contamination power of corpse impurity on: (1) graves; (2) persons; and (3) objects. It is important to note that contamination is conveyed by direct contact or by simply sharing an overhang with a corpse. For example, if individuals are simply in the same room as a corpse, they become impure even though they do not touch the corpse directly. (Num. 19; cf. m. *Oh* 3.1; 6.1; 11.4-6; t. *Oh.* 5.5).

2.1. Graves

In Second Temple times, graves were an impurity concern of the general Jewish population. Josephus notes the unwillingness of Jews to live in the newly constructed city of Tiberias, even though Herod offered them grants of houses and land. The reason: the city was built on grave sites (*Ant.* 18.38). The concern of contracting impurity from a grave is apparent among non-Jews as well. Greeks were afraid to step on a tomb and if a human bone or uncovered grave were discovered in a public place the area had to be purified (Parker 1983: 38–39).

Apparently, there was a practice of marking graves in Judaea so that they could be easily identified and avoided. Matthew refers to 'white-washed' graves, which may have been those marked with lime so that people could avoid them and not contract corpse impurity unnecessarily (Mt. 23.27; cf. Lk.11.44). According to the Mishnah, Jews marked graves so as not to become defiled by them (cf. m. *MQ* 1.2; b. *MQ* 5b). Corpse impurity was an important issue in the Second Temple era since corpse-contaminated individuals could not participate in worship at the sanctuary until they were purified.

The Rabbis provide more data concerning the potency of graves. According to the Mishnah, a grave contaminates a house built over it (m. *Oh.* 17.5). Corpse impurity was thought to penetrate upward through a grave, after which it was captured and contained by any structure built over it. The practice in many Christian churches of burying the dead under the sanctuary (cf. Westminster Abbey) would pose an unthinkable purity problem for Jews in antiquity. According to the Talmud, if a grave were discovered in a town, it had to be emptied (y. *Naz.* 9.3). According to R. Hisda, a grave outside of the city limits must be cleared if it is within 100 feet of the town. The Tosefta reduces this number to 75 feet and insists that even graves of kings and prophets must be removed (t. *BB* 1.11).

A field in which a grave is accidentally ploughed over contaminates for a

100-cubit radius from the grave, according to the Mishnah (m. *Oh.* 18.4). The soil in such a field must always be examined for bits of bone (m. *Oh* 18.4). If there are three or more corpses in the field, the area for 20 cubits in any direction away from the bodies is considered a graveyard and has to be avoided (m. *Oh.* 16.3). To purify an area in which a corpse had been found, one had first to remove the corpse, sift the soil for pieces of bone (m. *Oh.* 16.3-5), and then fill the field with new soil or overlay the old soil with paving stones (m. *Oh.* 18.5).

2.2. Persons

All persons who touch a corpse (even its blood or one of its bones) or share an overhang with it become impure for seven days (Num. 19.14). For example, if a person enters the house of death but does not touch the corpse, he or she still becomes impure for a week. This purificatory week requires special ablutions (see below). In turn, corpse-contaminated persons who do not purify themselves defile with a one-day impurity anyone who touches them (11Q19 50.8). The latter must bathe, launder and wait for sunset. Corpse impurity was considered contagious in other cultures as well. Among the Romans, for example, the entire *familia funesta*, the relatives of the dead, even if they lived in other towns and had not actually touched the corpse, became impure.

As noted above, the realm of the sacred was compromised cross-culturally in antiquity by the intrusion of the dead. The Temple Scroll is adamant on this point: corpse-contaminated individuals are not allowed to enter the holy city until they are completely purified (11Q19 45.17; 49.21; cf. Num. 5.2). Separate areas were established for them outside the Temple city during their week of purification. In the case of ordinary cities, corpse-contaminated persons were not expelled but were quarantined within the city. During this week of purification, the purifying person was allowed to eat ordinary food but not the *tohorah*, pure food (11Q19 49.20-21; 4Q514 4–7).

As stated earlier, a pregnant woman who miscarries is, according to the Temple Scroll, impure. As long as the dead foetus remains within her, it renders her impure like a grave (11Q19 50.11). As a 'grave', she contaminates every house she enters and renders its contents impure requiring the week of purification described below. Those who touch her become impure for one day. Those who enter a house with her become impure for seven days. This law, in particular, reveals the bias of the sect towards greater severity, and this is brought into relief when compared with Rabbinic interpretation: 'If the foetus dies in its mother's womb and the midwife places her hand inside and touches it, the midwife remains impure for seven days, but the mother remains pure until the foetus comes out of her' (i.e. just like a woman giving birth, m. *Ḥul.* 4.3). The Rabbis treat a woman who miscarries just like a woman giving birth in that she does not become impure until the foetus emerges. According to the sectarians, on the other hand, such a woman contains a corpse.[1] The Rabbis do not classify the foetus in the womb as a separate being. A miscarriage then cannot be classified as a corpse since it was never alive.

There were at least two levels of purity among the sectarians. In more than one text, there is a distinction between the ordinary member of the sect and the more scrupulous person. For example, the Temple Scroll regards eating the contents of sealed vessels in the house of death as permissible but notes that the 'pure man' (*'ish tahor*) will avoid even this because it has been in a corpse-contaminated house (11Q19 49.8). Cave 4 fragment 274 (3.ii) makes a similar distinction between the ordinary person and the *tahor yoter*, 'more pure person'. Like the Temple Scroll, 4Q274 suggests that a purer person will not eat the contents of even a sealed vessel in the house of the dead (4Q274 3; 11Q19 49.8). Scripture, on the other hand, is quite clear that it is the 'open' vessel in the house of death which receives impurity into its contents (Num. 19.15). The implication is that if the vessels had been sealed, they would have protected their contents from impurity.[2] The Damascus Document provides another example of this distinction. It differentiates between the men of 'perfect holiness' and the rest (CD 7.5-6).

To be sure, there is already a two-tier system with regard to corpse impurity in Scripture: the law pertaining to the priests and the law pertaining to laity. Priests can only attend the burial of immediate relatives (cf. Lev. 21.2-3, wife is not included). According to Ezekiel, the priest who handles a corpse becomes impure for 15 days, not just one week, and he must bring a sacrifice at the close of this period in order to expunge his impurity (Ezek. 44.26-27). The Qumran sect, many of whom had no doubt functioned as priests in the Temple (see Chapter 1), often exhibit this more stringent stance toward impurity. The High Priest should not have any contact with death, not even to bury his parents. A more stringent priestly attitude to corpse impurity is reflected among non-Jewish priests as well. Solon tradition prohibits any priest from attending a

1. The sect considers the foetus a separate life: (1) 11Q19 50.10-19 considers the dead foetus a corpse inside the mother, (2) an animal found alive inside the womb of a slaughtered animal requires separate slaughter (4QMMT B36–38; cf. also 11Q19 52.5-7; 4Q270 9 ii 15, Baumgarten 1995a: 445–48).

2. The Rabbis make the further deduction that since the sealed vessel appears unaffected by the corpse impurity, earthenware must receive impurity only via its interior (*Sif. shem. sher. par.* 7.5; *Sif. meṣ. zab. par.* 3.2).

funeral. The Hellenistic Syrian priest is defiled for an entire day merely for looking at a corpse (Lucian 2.62; Attridge and Oden 1976: 57). All sacred personnel, objects and areas take on greater susceptibility to corpse impurity.

2.3. Objects

Like persons, susceptible objects are subject to contamination by contact with death. According to Num. 19.14, everything in the tent of a dead person automatically becomes impure for seven days. Yet Num. 19.15 adds the curious statement that any open vessel becomes unclean. The Rabbis infer from this verse that closed vessels and other items in the tent of the dead do not become unclean; sealed vessels retain their purity and protect their contents. We will see below that the sectarians would disagree.

The types of objects susceptible to corpse impurity are interpreted maximally at Qumran. According to the Damascus Document, all vessels of wood, stones and dust within the house of the dead could transmit impurity if moistened with oil (CD 12.15-17; Ginzberg 1976: 81–82, 115; Eshel 2000: 48). Also susceptible in the house of death are 'any vessel, nail, or peg in a wall', thus reflecting a stringent code (CD 12.17-18). Likewise, the Temple Scroll maintains that every lock and lintel in a corpse-contaminated house is impure (11Q19 49.13). Not only the contents but also the house itself is impure for seven days (11Q19 49.5-6). Walls, doors and floors must be scraped (11Q19 49.12). This follows from Num. 19.18 which states that the tent itself must be sprinkled.

The strict, literalist bias of the Qumran sect comes into further relief when susceptible items are contrasted with Rabbinic interpretation. First, the Rabbis limit the impurity inside the house of the dead to the contents of open vessels; if the vessel is sealed both it and its contents remain pure. Second, the Rabbis limit the susceptible *kelim* to items made of the materials listed in Leviticus in the context of impurity: earthenware, leather and fabric (m. *Kel.* 15.1; Lev. 11.32).[3] Metal is also included because of Scripture's reference to the defiling quality of the sword of the slain (Num. 19.16; b. *Hul.* 2b–3a; b. *Pes.* 14ab) and the purification of the Israelites' metal vessels after the war with the Midianites (Num. 31.22-23). Third, since Scripture qualifies susceptible *kelim* as items 'with which

3. According to the Rabbis, if the item is made of clay, it must be broken unless it is sealed. For the sectarians, even a sealed vessel becomes impure. Objects made of other materials are impure for seven days and must undergo purification rites. This distinction may be based on the porous nature of earthenware which might absorb some impurity that water could not expunge (Gray 1903: 40).

any work is done' (Lev. 11.32), these items must form complete, usable vessels (m. *Kel.* 2.1; *Sif. Num.* 126[162]).

The Rabbis differ strikingly from the Qumran exegetes by limiting the effect of corpse impurity. The Rabbis render the tent and its contents impure only if they are made of the particular items listed above. In addition, the item must be, like a tent, unattached to the ground (b. *Shab.* 81a); houses and other permanent buildings are insusceptible. The sectarians take a more stringent approach. Probably the case of the leprous house is their model. Since the stones of a leprous house must be removed, houses and stone are thus, in the sectarian opinion, susceptible to impurity, i.e. all types of impurity including corpse impurity. The Karaites and Josephus concur with the sectarians that a house qualifies as a tent.[4]

Liquids play a strong role in conveying impurity in both the Qumran and Rabbinic systems (see Chapter 1), and this is especially evident in the house of the dead. According to the Temple Scroll, the house of the dead must be swept clean of all oil, wine and water moisture (11Q19 49.11-14). The Damascus Document concurs and states that oil stains on vessels of wood, stones or dust convey impurity (CD 12.14-18; Baumgarten 1977: 91). This attitude is confirmed by Josephus who says that elder members of the sect who have anointed themselves with oil become impure when they touch junior members (*War* 2.150). In this case, it is the moisture of the oil which conveys impurity. In fact, due to the large number of stone vessels found at Qumran, H. Eshel (2000: 52) argues that stone vessels were susceptible to impurity only if oil was on them. Otherwise, as in the Rabbinic view, stone vessels did protect their contents.

The potency of liquids probably has both biblical and physical roots. According to Lev. 11.38, water which is put on a crop (whether by rain, dew or irrigation) renders it susceptible to impurity; if the produce remains dry, however, no impurity can be conveyed to it. This is not only a biblical command but follows logically from nature. It is when soil is moistened that it smears and renders persons and objects physically unclean. The same reasoning is easily applied to ritual impurity as well.

4. In one way the Rabbis are more stringent in the matter of corpse impurity than the sectarians. The large part of *Ohalot* is concerned with tents, containers housing corpse matter. According to the Mishnah, a 'tent', is any susceptible 'tent-like' container which defiles its contents, though it excludes houses. And an overhang could simply be the shade of a tree. Nevertheless, for all practical purposes, the Rabbis have still limited the effect of corpse impurity by excluding the actual house of the dead, the most likely place to find a corpse, from susceptibility. It is difficult to draw the line between Rabbinic academics and actual practice.

3. Purification

The Torah sets forth a specific ritual for purifying those contaminated by a corpse. A mixture of spring water and the ash of a specially consecrated red cow was to be sprinkled on the impure person/object on the third and seventh days of impurity (Num 19.18f). Corpse-contaminated individuals had to bathe and launder their clothes at the end of the seven days (Num 19.19).

A first-century Jewish writer, Josephus, warns that anyone who does not purify after seven days of corpse impurity must bring a sacrifice to the Temple to atone for this transgression (*Ant.* 3.262). Thus, even if not planning to visit the Temple, a corpse-contaminated individual had to purify after the week's period of impurity (cf. also Num. 19.20). In this period, corpse impurity was a widespread concern among both Jews and non-Jews and, at least in Jewish circles, affected both priests and laity (Alon 1977: 190–234; Regev 2000b: 176; *contra* Sanders 1990: 134–254).

3.1. Red Cow Ritual

How does one obtain the special purification ash? Scripture outlines a procedure in which an unblemished red cow was slaughtered outside the camp in a clean place, its blood sprinkled towards the Temple, and its ashes preserved in a pure location to be used later for purification of those with corpse impurity (Num. 19.9). The ritual was clearly considered a sacred rite, since the cow is called a *ḥatta't*, purification offering, and a consecrated priest sprinkled some of the cow's blood in the direction of the sanctuary seven times, thus linking the burning of the animal with the holy altar (Milgrom 1981: 67). Cedarwood, hyssop and scarlet wool were thrown into the conflagration. The redness of these items is symbolic of the cow's red blood which is the purgative agent. The ashes of the cow were then collected and deposited in a clean place. According to the Mishnah, the procedure took place on the Mount of Olives (m. *Par.* 3.6).

The Pharisees and Sadducees of the Mishnah argued over the correct standard of purity for those who participated in the red cow rite. The Sadducees, who did not regard a purifying person as pure until sunset, would not let any such person participate, and in this case, the Qumran sectarians would have sided with them (4Q277 1 ii 2). This insistence on full purification before functioning within society surfaces in several Qumran texts and is a distinctive trait of the community (cf. also 4Q266 9 ii 1-4; MMT B 13–17; 11Q19 51.2-5).

The sanctity of the rite was upheld by the Qumran authors (cf. m. *Par.* 2.3). The sect required that only priests perform all parts of the rite, including collection of ash and disposal of the blood. The author of

Miqṣat Ma'aśe ha-Torah corroborates the biblical designation that the red cow is a sacrifice, a *ḥatta't* (MMT B 13). 4Q276 requires the vessel which contains the cow's blood to be first sanctified at the Temple altar (4Q276 3; cf. b. *Zeb.* 20b). The slaughterer, the burner, the collecter of the ash, and the one who sprinkles the purification water must be completely pure before participating in the rite. Curiously, the priestly garments are not allowed for use in this rite. This may be, as Baumgarten suggests, simply due to the fact that the rite is not conducted at the Temple, or it may be that the author did not want the holy vestments to become defiled (Baumgarten, private communication; also cf. Baumgarten 1999b: 112).

The Qumran texts authenticate the red cow ritual for the period of the Second Temple (cf. also *Ep. Barn.* 8.1). The Mishnah claims that only a few red cows were burned in Jewish history, but since only a minimal amount of ash was required to make the purgation water, the ashes of an entire cow would last a long time (m. *Par.* 3.5). The Jerusalem Talmud records instances of Rabbis using the red cow ash for corpse purification (y. *Ber.* 6.10a). The Samaritans are reported to have used it until the fourteenth century. They continued to sprinkle the purgation water in the direction of their sanctuary even after its demise.

3.2. Purification Procedures

According to the sectarians at Qumran, corpse-contaminated persons were barred from eating of the communal 'purity' and had to undergo a week-long purification process. They were required to immerse themselves in water on the first day of impurity lest their touch cause impurity to others (11Q19 49.16-17; cf. 50.13-14; 1QM 14.2-3). On days three and seven of the purification week they were sprinkled with water mixed with ashes of the red cow prepared as described above. They were not considered pure until sunset on the seventh day. At the end of this time, they immersed again and recited a blessing to God (4Q277, lines 7-9; 4Q284 frag. 2; 4Q512). Immersion before prayer appears to be the norm in the Second Temple period (cf. T. Levi 2.3; Jdt. 12.7).

While Scripture mandates the sprinkling of purgation water by a hyssop sprig on days three and seven of corpse contamination, there is disagreement among later interpreters over who should be involved in the sprinkling. The Mishnah seems to imply that the Rabbis allowed young boys to sprinkle the corpse-contaminated (m. *Par.* 3.2-4). The idea may have been that young boys would be pure from sexual emissions and thus fit to purify the impure. In any case, the Tohorot author insists that only a mature priest be allowed this privilege (Baumgarten 1995b: 112–19). Here the reasoning seems to be that an adult would be more trustworthy in maintaining purity while conducting the rite and, as with the participants in the red cow ritual, only a priest would be holy enough to counteract the impurity involved: 'Only a priest who is pure shall sprinkle [upon] them, fo[r] he [is pur]ging the impu[re]' (4Q277 1 ii 6-7).

Objects which were contaminated by corpse impurity were sprinkled with the special purgation water on the third and seventh days of their impurity. The Torah prescribes the sprinkling of everything which had been within the tent of the corpse (Num. 19.18). In addition, all vessels which could withstand it had to be purified by fire; those which could not endure the fire had to at least be passed through water (Num. 31.23). The intensity of this impurity is evident in the purification required.

According to the Temple Scroll everything in a corpse-contaminated house is unclean for seven days (11Q19 49). Particular items are mentioned: wet food is unclean, drink is unclean, clay pots must be broken, and open vessels spoil their contents. Cooking utensils, e.g. mills, mortars and pots, are washed. Vessels of any substance, including, wood, stone or metal are susceptible, as well as, clothes, sacks and skins. Purgation water was sprinkled on days three and seven preceded in each case by immersion of the unclean item.

Impure stains from liquids, e.g. stains of oil, wine and water, have to be removed, according to several scrolls found at Qumran (Baumgarten 1967: 183–93; Eshel 2000: 45). It is well known that liquids were a strong purity concern at Qumran because access to communal drinks was granted to the novitiate at Qumran only after two to three years of probation (1QS 6.20; 7.20; cf. *War* 2.123). According to the Damascus Document, oil stains in the house of the dead had to be removed so that corpse impurity would not spread (CD 12.15-17). The Temple Scroll insists that all liquid, even water stains, in such a house becomes impure and must be removed (11Q19 49.8-11). Thus, in addition to purifying the items listed above, the sectarians rubbed floors, walls, doors, hinges, jambs and lintels.

Several Qumran Scrolls require an immersion of the corpse-impure person on the first day of the purifying week (11Q19 49.17; 4Q414 2 ii 2; 4Q514). This allows the person to eat ordinary food although he still may not mingle with the community. There may be a biblical hint of this Qumran practice in Lev.19.18 where the corpse-contaminated person is at home undergoing purification. According to Num 5.2, the corpse-contaminated person is expelled from the city, but perhaps an initial immersion on the first day allowed the impure person to stay at home to finish the purificatory week. In any case, the Qumran version is clear that in order for the purifying person to eat even profane food, he must immerse (4Q514; 4Q274).

There is substantial support for an initial first-day bathing after exposure to corpse impurity among Jews in Second Temple times (Eshel

1997: 8–10). A good example is Tobit, who washed himself on the evening of his first day of corpse impurity (Tob. 2.9). Philo states that the corpse-impure had to purify themselves on the first day of their impurity. According to him, such persons were not allowed to touch anything until they had first bathed and laundered their clothes (*De Specialibus Legibus* 3.206-207). In addition, *miqva'ot* have been found at cemeteries in Judaea: (1) at the tombs of Helena of Adiabene, and (2) in the courtyard of a burial cave at Jericho (Kon 1947: 31–38; Reich 1980: 251–53; Hachlili and Killebrew 1983: 112).

The requirement of an immediate purification after contact with the dead produces an early version of the Rabbinic *tebul yom*, a purifying person who has immersed and is simply waiting for sunset for purification to be complete. The individual is not completely purified but is pure enough to function within ordinary society. Corpse-impure persons remain barred from sacred places and items until completely purified.

There is an important difference between the Rabbinic and Qumranic attitudes. For the Rabbis the *tebul yom* is a pure man for almost all intents and purposes. For example, the Rabbis refer to the man gathering the ash as an *'ish tahor* 'pure man' (*Sif. Num.* on Numbers 19). This person is clearly not completely pure since, although he has immersed, he has not waited until sunset before gathering the ash. For the Qumran sectarians, the person waiting for complete purification still remains decidedly within the *impure* category (4Q266 9 ii 4; 4Q276–77; 11Q19 51.2-5; MMT B 13–17). For the Rabbis, life would simply be too difficult if every purifying person had to wait until sunset before going about mundane business.

The Sabbath, according to 4Q274, overrides all purification procedures. The writer is concerned that someone in the middle of his purification week will violate the Sabbath by the sprinkling procedure (4Q274 2 i). That person should (1) make sure not to touch any purities during the Sabbath, and (2) wait until the Sabbath is over for the second sprinkling.

Finally, the purification process includes blessings to be recited by the purifying person. Both 4Q512 and 4Q414, although fragments, record the blessings, both before and after purification, which the purifying person is obliged to offer. The purifying person confesses his sins, asks for forgiveness and then thanks God for his mercy. Apparently, the purification blessing is made after immersion and after the purifying person puts his clothes on (cf. 4Q512 12 x). By contrast, the Rabbinic blessings, recited after ritual purification, are not linked with sins.

One of the most explicit examples of ritual purification with penitence attached is found in the purifying process of the corpse-contaminated individual. 4Q512 clearly refers to an individual who is purifying after contact with the dead, since the special 'third day' purification is mentioned. The purification week with special ablutions on days one, three and seven is distinctly that of the corpse-impure person as discussed above. But in 4Q512, this individual thanks God particularly for *kippur*, atonement from guilt. (See Chapter 1 for further discussion of this phenomenon.)

Me niddah is the purgation water which was sprinkled on the corpse-impure on days three and seven of the week of impurity. The term *me niddah*, comes from the verbal root *nazah*, 'to spatter' and so means 'water for sprinkling, water for lustration' (Levine 1993: 274–75). This special purgation water may have been used at Qumran for other impurities besides corpse impurity (see Chapter 1). In any case, *me niddah* was most likely in addition to, not in place of, immersion. Scripture mandates that the corpse-contaminated person be sprinkled with the special water/ash mixture as well as immerse in water (Num. 19.19; 4Q277 1 ii 8-10). In fact, there is sufficient evidence that those persons impure from any major biblical impurity had to immerse in water, sometimes in addition to other forms of purification, e.g. washing hands, sacrifices, and sprinklings of blood and/or *me niddah* (Milgrom 1991: 667, 934–35).

Apparently *me niddah* was used to purify pilgrims before festivals, at least according to sectarian doctrine. 4Q414 mentions 'those purified for his fixed times', showing that purification before festivals was required. The Laws for Purification 4Q284 (or Purification Liturgy), fragment 1, a text which begins in the middle of a discussion of the festal calendar, includes *me niddah* in the purification necessary to participate in these festivals. Apparently, since the layperson would be entering the sanctuary courts, there is a concern that corpse impurity may be present. Before the festival was an appropriate time for individuals to make sure of their purity and especially to purify unattended corpse impurity (cf. Ezek. 36.25).

4. Significance

The impurity of the dead is the most potent of all impurities throughout the ancient world, among Jews as well as pagans. God is the God of the living and the dead cannot praise him, according to the Psalmist. Pagan gods are considered by the Rabbis to be no gods at all, and idols are associated with the impurity of a dead creature (m. *AZ* 3.6; b. *AZ*). Josephus explains that the soul suffers in the body of impure persons just as it does at the point of death (*Ag. Ap.* 2.203). These attitudes are similarly confirmed at Qumran. It is very likely that corpse purification with its special purgation water, was used to mark the very entrance of a candidate to the sect: he passed from death to life by his entrance into the community.

The Scrolls describe corpse impurity in more stringent terms than can be found in any other Jewish group in antiquity. Corpse impurity was potent enough to defile all of the contents of a house, even doors, floors, locks and lintels. Persons who were contaminated by a corpse or even entered a house of death were contagious to other persons and objects and could cause them to become impure. Thus, the sect apparently barred all persons who were corpse-impure from participation within the sect's communal activities. According to the Temple Scroll, separate shelters were constructed outside of the Temple City and within the ordinary city for those impure from a corpse. Other texts require corpse-contaminated persons to bathe on the first day of impurity just in order to eat their own food; they still cannot eat the communal meal. This stands in contrast to the attitude of the Rabbis, who allowed the purifying person to participate in society in all matters except those dealing with sancta.

Purification was essential according to the sectarians, but it is unclear how they accomplished it at Qumran. No evidence of the red cow ritual has been found nor is it likely that it would have been conducted out of sight of the Temple. Probably, as with all other sacrificial rites, this one was held in abeyance until the sect could regain control of the Jerusalem cult. Indeed, they had specific ideas on how corpse impurity was to be handled in their future restoration.

At Qumran, corpse impurity carries a further stain than in other ancient Jewish systems. The corpse-contaminated person pleads for God's mercy to restore him to his former status. There is a sense that he is somehow unacceptable from a moral point of view until he is purified. This process is not automatic but requires soul-searching and humility and ultimately depends on God's grace. The association of guilt and corpse impurity is found, to my knowledge, nowhere else in early Jewish sources.

5. Appendix: Carcass

A *nebelah*, or carcass, is a dead animal which is either (1) in the Torah's list of forbidden animals for food; or (2) a permitted animal for food which has not been properly slaughtered. The Qumran sectarians interpret both of these categories expansively.

The Temple Scroll reiterates the Torah's list of impure creatures. Accordingly, Israel may eat of winged insects: locust, bald locust, cricket and grasshopper (11Q19 48). These crawl on four legs and their hind legs are larger than their forelegs, enabling them to leap; they also fly. All creepers are unclean, including the mouse, rat and lizard (11Q19 50). Israel must never eat any carcass, but carcasses could be sold to Gentiles.

There is ambiguity in Scripture as to the law regarding *nebelah* and *terefah*. The latter is an animal which has been injured, e.g. as prey of another animal. Deuteronomy forbids eating *nebelah* but is silent with regard to *terefah* (Deut. 14.20–21). Leviticus states that eating of either category incurs a one-day impurity but the text does not expressly forbid it (Lev. 17.15). Exodus forbids eating prey but says nothing about an animal which has died of old age (Exod. 22.30). Qumran combines all of these accounts in typically severe fashion, requiring that both *nebelah* and *terefah* be discarded (4Q251 12.3-5; Baumgarten 1999b: 40–41; cf. b. *Men.* 45a).

The consequences of handling carcasses are serious. Those who touch them must bathe, launder their clothes and wait for sunset (11Q19 51). This affects not only those who carry the entire carcass but even those who merely handle a bone, skin, flesh or even claws. This contrasts with the Rabbinic view, which is more lenient. According to the Rabbis, animal bones, skin, claws and horns do not defile (m. *Hul.* 9.1). Curiously, jars of animal bones have been discovered at Qumran.

The Temple City required a more restricted definition of 'proper slaughter'. The flesh of an animal carcass was unacceptable for food and its hide was forbidden for use unless it had first been sacrificed on the altar. According to both the Temple Scroll and MMT, these animals had first to be slaughtered as sacrifices within the city before they could be used (11Q19 51.1-6; 4QMMT B 21–26).[5] No profane slaughtering was allowed within three days' distance of the Temple. The animals had to be offered as sacrifices and eaten within the sacred environs. In ordinary cities proper slaughter meant that the blood of the animal was poured out on the ground and covered with dust (11Q19 53). Since blood represented the life of the animal and also the means of atonement in Israel, it had to be handled carefully (Lev. 17.11; cf. also *Jubilees*' great concern for disposal of blood).

The rationale for these laws reiterates a theme of Leviticus stated repeatedly in the Temple Scroll: 'Because I, the LORD, reside among the

5. One reading of *Ant.* 18.18-19 suggests that the Essenes did not shun sacrifice but simply sacrificed separately at the Jerusalem Temple (Baumgarten 1977: 62). Josephus also refers to an Essene gate in Jerusalem, *Bethso* (*War* 5.145). Strict ideas of slaughter and sacrifice, like those represented here in the Temple Scroll, possibly gave rise to separate, incompatible practices.

children of Israel. You shall sanctify them and they shall be holy.' As with other purity topics, so also with the carcass: not only the area of the sacred is guarded against impurity, but profane areas as well. On one level, the sanctity of the Temple reaches out to restrict the entire city of the Temple and, on another level, the presence of the sacred city in the land increases the level of purity required for ordinary cities.

Further Reading

Baumgarten, J.M.
1995b 'The Red Cow Purification Rites in Qumran Texts', *JJS* 46: 112–19.

Douglas, M.
1993 *In the Wilderness: The Doctrine of Defilement in the Book of Numbers* (Sheffield: Sheffield Academic Press).

Eshel, E.
1997 '4Q414 Fragment 2: Purification of a Corpse-Contaminated Person', in *Legal Texts and Legal Issues: The Proceedings of the Second Meeting of the International Organization for Qumran Studies, published in honor of Joseph M. Baumgarten* (Leiden: E.J. Brill): 3–10.

Eshel, H.
2000 'CD 12.15–17 and the Stone Vessels found at Qumran', in *The Damascus Document: A Centennial of Discovery*, ed. J.M. Baumgarten *et al.* (Leiden: E.J. Brill): 45–52.

Hachlili, R.
2000 'Cemeteries', in *Encyclopedia of the Dead Sea Scrolls*, I, eds. L.H. Schiffman and J.C. VanderKam (Oxford: Oxford University Press): 125–29.

Hachlili, R. and A. Killebrew
1983 'Jewish Funerary Customs during the Second Temple Period in Light of the Excavations at the Jericho Necropolis', *PEQ* 115: 109–39.

Schiffman, L.H.
1990a 'The Impurity of the Dead in the Temple Scroll', in *Archaeology and History in the Dead Sea Scrolls*, ed. L.H. Schiffman (Sheffield: JSOT Press): 135–56.

4

LEPROSY

1. Definition

The Scrolls use two terms to refer to the leper: *menuga*ʿ and *meṣora*ʿ. The term *menuga*ʿ is a general term for a person with a *nega*ʿ, some type of plague (Exod. 11.1; 1 Kgs. 8.37–38; Ps. 91.10; cf. Gen. 12.17; Ps. 73.5, 14). The root of *menuga*ʿ and *nega*ʿ is *naga*ʿ, which literally means 'becoming touched'. In the ancient near east, leprosy was a sign that someone had 'become touched' by a demon. In the Bible, too, skin disease, *meṣora*ʿ, was often a sign that God was angry with a person and had 'touched', i.e. punished, him in this way. Scripture, however, never describes leprosy as the work of demons; God is always the author and controller of the disease. Unlike other cultures in the near east, leprosy in Israel is not a matter for exorcists. The appropriate response from the afflicted person is repentance and a plea for mercy from God. Only if divine healing is granted can the purification process begin through the agency of a priest.

*Meṣora*ʿ, from the root *ṣara*ʿ, is a more specific term for the leper than *menuga*ʿ. *Ṣara*ʿ*at*, usually translated 'leprosy' is a biblical term for a variety of skin diseases, and the passive participle *ṣaru*ʿ*a* is the Scroll authors' preferred way of saying 'leprous'. A more accurate translation of *ṣara*ʿ*at* is 'scale disease' because the particular symptoms of the disease described in Scripture entail the flaking of the skin. Symptoms of leprosy according to Leviticus 13–14 include: *se'et*, discoloration; *sappaḫat*, scab; *baheret*, shiny mark (Lev. 13.2). Any significant change in skin or hair, e.g. penetration of an affection beneath the skin, discoloration and spread of the affected area, or ulceration of the skin, signals a case of leprosy (Wilkinson 1977: 155–60; Milgrom 1991: 773). If the disease causes hair within the affected area to turn white, it is *ṣara*ʿ*at*. If the disease involves only a discoloration on the surface of the skin, it is considered a minor irritation like eczema or psoriasis and not *ṣaraʿat*. However, if it penetrates through the epidermis to the dermis, it is diagnosed as leprosy (Rabinowitz 1971: 33–34). *Ṣaraʿat* could occur at any time but certain circumstances are pointed out by Leviticus as especially conducive to the eruption of the disease: namely, following a boil (13.18-23) or burn (13.24-28). The disease could also break out on a beard turning the hair yellow and thin (13.29-37), or even on a bald head as a scaly rash (13.42-44).

How was scale disease ascertained? The Scrolls, based on biblical prescription, insist that only a priest has the authority to declare that a person is a leper (Lev. 14.30). If he is a simpleton, the Inspector will instruct him (CD 13.5-6). The Rabbis agree that only a priest may declare the disease, and they describe the way in which a priest should be instructed: 'They say to him [the priest], "Say, Impure", and he says "Impure"; "Say, Pure", and he says, "Pure" ' (m. *Neg.* 3.1). The Tosefta adds, 'If one is not an expert in them [plagues] and their names, he should not examine the plagues' (t. *Neg.* 1.1). The Qumran sectarians emphasize the need for the priest; the Rabbis emphasize the manner of instructing the priest. Nevertheless, both groups agree that only a priest, even if he is ignorant, may make the declaration; they differ only with regard to emphasis.

According to the Bible, a person who developed a shiny mark on the skin was quarantined to see whether or not the affliction would deepen and turn hair white (Lev. 13.3). If there was improvement and the mark went away, the person was released. If the matter stayed the same, the person was quarantined for another week. Then, if the symptoms faded, the person was released after purification, i.e. bathing and laundering. If the symptoms remained the same or spread, the person was certified as a *meṣoraʿ* and banished from the community. Curiously, if all the hair on a person's body turned white, the individual was declared pure. The cause was something other than leprosy.

The Damascus Document goes over the inspection process of a person suspected of having scale disease (4Q267 9 i; 4Q271 7). Yellow, unnourished hair is a warning sign of possible impurity. If this condition spreads, resulting in much yellow dead hair on the scalp, the afflicted person is diagnosed by the priest as impure. If, on the other hand, the condition improves 'and the artery is full of blood, and the *spirit of life* goes up and down through it, the disease is healed'. Blood is equated with life (Lev. 17.11) and thus the renewal of circulating blood on the individual's head indicates the spirit of life.

In a case where no hair is involved, the priest examines the skin. If dead skin is not deeper than the living skin the suspected leper is confined until the flesh grows. If the 'spirit of life' goes up and down in the rash after one week, it is cured. If the rash is deeper than the skin, leprosy has taken hold of the living skin (cf. 4Q272).

Leprosy can also occur among fabrics and houses. In this case, *ṣaraʿat* refers to probably fungus or mildew, which discolours the stones in the house and spreads throughout it, contaminating both the house and its contents. Quarantine of fabrics and houses is similar to that of persons. Any evidence of fungus subjects the item to a seven-day quarantine. If no improvement can be ascertained after this week, the priest pronounces the house or garment impure. All affected stones are thrown outside the city and replaced (14.40-42). If the disease spreads throughout the house, the entire building has to be torn down (14.43-45). The Sifre Midrash Moshe makes reference to a leprous house, but the material is too fragmented to yield much information.

2. Contamination

Unlike modern leprosy, i.e. Hansen's Disease, *ṣaraʿat* is not considered medically contagious. The symptoms described above are not generally transferrable to other persons. Note that Naaman, the Syrian leper of 2 Kgs 5.1, was able to function as a military commander in close contact with an army of men. Also, strangely enough, in the event that symptoms of *ṣaraʿat* cover the entire body, the individual is pronounced clean! The matter is more of a ritual concern than one of physical health.

Although not physically contagious, scale disease is nevertheless the most ritually contagious of all impurities in the biblical system, except for corpse impurity (cf. Gentile rankings of different degrees of impurity: m. *Kel.* 1.3; m. *Zab.* 5.6-7). According to the Temple Scroll, the leper cannot enter any city until purified (11Q19 48.14-15). The author describes a special quarantine area east of the Temple City reserved for lepers as well as separate areas for certain other types of impurity bearers (11Q19 46.16-18). The Scrolls and the Mishnah forbid lepers to enter other walled cities as well (11Q19 48.14; 4Q274 1.1-2; m. *Kel.* 1.7; cf. Num. 5.2). No contact is allowed with them (cf. *Ant.* 3.264; *Ag. Ap.* 1.281). Ostracized from society, the leper's daily existence was miserable.

The language of 4QTohorot, fragment 1, is reminiscent of Scripture's prescriptions regarding the leper who must reside apart (*badad yeshev*) from other persons and call out 'Impure, impure' to all who pass by (4Q274 1.1-3; Lev. 13.45-46; Milgrom 1991: 806). Nevertheless, this passage may be referring to the *zab* since it focuses on the contamination of the individual's bed and seat, and continues with prescriptions for the *zabah* and other persons with bodily discharges (see Chapter 5, Bodily

Discharges; Baumgarten 1999b: 101). Indeed, the leper can be described as a visibly decaying person, the 'living dead', as it were (see below under 'Significance').

The Gospels support the notion that lepers were not made to live all that far from the rest of the population. A *meṣoraʿ*, who had probably been cured, gave lodging to Jesus in Bethany, a small town on the outskirts of Jerusalem (Mk 14.3). Apparently, lepers did not come near pure individuals. Ten lepers desiring Jesus' attention stood at a distance so as not to defile him (Lk. 17.11-19; cf. also Mk 1.40-45; Lk. 7.22).

The Qumran sectarians share with the later Rabbis the idea of isolating the leper even from other impure individuals. According to the Tohorot texts, 'Impure, impure' was also translated, 'Impure to the impure' (4Q274 1.3). The same notion underlies the talmudic interpretation of '*badad yeshev*, alone shall he dwell' (Lev. 13.46). The Rabbis explain that the passage forbids any other impure persons to reside with the leper (b. *Pes.* 67a). Indeed, the Gospels include many stories about lepers, and, while they may live with other lepers, they never appear in conjunction with other types of impure persons (cf. Lk. 17.11-19). Apparently, even in the larger Jewish world, impure persons can contract even greater impurity if they make contact with an unclean person or item. According to the Scrolls, all impure persons who make any further contact with impurity are required to perform ablutions before eating any food whatever (cf. 4Q274; 4Q514; Baillet 1982: 296). They would, of course, still be barred from communal meal and have to eat separately (4Q514; Milgrom 1994a: 177).

What is the extent of contamination by the leper? Here the Scrolls are silent and our knowledge is based on the biblical example of the leprous house and its Rabbinic interpretation. All who lie down or eat in a leprous house are required to bathe and launder their clothes (Lev. 13.47). From the data regarding the leprous house, as well as the analogy of the leper to the corpse, the Rabbis regard the overhang of any ceiling, awning or tent as conveying the impurity of a leper under it to persons and susceptible items sharing the overhang. A person sharing an overhang with a leper must bathe, and anyone who stays under the overhang and lies down or eats there must launder as well (m. *Neg.* 13.7-9). It is most likely that the Scroll authors similarly ascribed to the leper's contagion by overhang.

Cave 4 fragments certainly regard physical contact with impure persons as defiling, and they acknowledge the leper's warning, 'Impure, impure' (4Q274). Scripture says this call is spoken with a covered mouth (Lev. 13.45), probably so that the leper's saliva and breath could not come into contact with pure persons passing by (b. *MQ* 15a; y. *BB* 3.9; *Lev. R.* 16.3;

Maimonides *Code* X, 10.6). His appearance, dishevelled hair and torn clothes, would, of course, also warn bystanders of his presence.

At first glance, it may appear that the Rabbis increase the potency of leprosy in Israel; their explication of the contamination power of this disease is detailed. However, the opposite is true. The Mishnah defines leprosy so narrowly that it is almost impossible to state with certainty that a person has the disease. The Rabbis limit the disease to the symptom of *baheret*, the bright spot, defined in modern terms as vitiligo, or leuce, a very rare skin disease (Rabinowitz 1971: 38). The Scroll authors, by contrast, make no effort to restrict the definition of *ṣaraʿat*. Although they are silent on the matter of overhang, it is clear already from Scripture that the disease, ritually speaking, is exceptionally contagious.

3. Purification

According to Scripture, after a leper is healed he must undergo an eight-day purification ritual. On the first day, the priest meets him outside the camp for inspection. If the leper is indeed healed, the priest kills a bird and dips a bunch of hyssop, cedarwood, crimson wool and a live bird into the dead bird's blood. The priest sprinkles the purifying leper with the blood mixed with running water, *mayim ḥayyim*, seven times, and then releases the remaining bird. The purifying leper shaves his hair, bathes and launders his clothes. He remains outside the community for one more week and then repeats the shaving, bathing and laundering, after which he is re-admitted to his home. On the eighth day he offers concluding sacrifices (whole burnt, cereal, purification and reparation) with meal and oil accompaniments at the sanctuary. The priest daubs his right ear, hand and foot with sacrificial blood and oil, and then pronounces the leper pure. The seventh-day purification admits the leper to the lay, profane sphere and the eighth-day sacrifices admit him to the sanctuary and the holy sphere.

According to the Scrolls, individuals who are purifying themselves from leprosy must not touch any impurity. Purifying lepers who touch any impure person are not allowed to eat until they first bathe and launder their clothes. Furthermore, a purifying leper is not supposed to touch pure persons lest the latter be defiled. According to the Temple Scroll, the purifying leper who touches a pure person contaminates the latter (11Q19 49.19-21). In fact, this can be deduced already from Scripture. According to Lev. 14 the purifying leper first bathes, shaves his hair and launders his clothes, and then is allowed into the city, but he must remain outside of the house for seven days. Perhaps the reason that the purifying leper must stay outside of his house is that he will contaminate some of the contents of the house, especially sacred food (Milgrom 1991: 993). MMT seems to reflect this line of reasoning when the author complains: '[The leper] shall dwell outside his tent seven d]ays. But now [i.e. outside Qumran] while their impurity is [still] with them [lepers are entering] into the house [constaining] the purity of sacred [food]' (4QMMT B 66–68).

According to the sectarians, the impurity of leprosy takes longer to purify than according to the Rabbis. The purifying leper is not allowed to eat sacred food until sunset on the eighth day (MMT B 71–72). For the Rabbis, by contrast, the process is complete when sacrifices are offered on the eighth day at the Temple (m. *Neg.* 14.3). There is no need to wait until sunset.

4. Significance

Throughout the ancient world, both pagan and Jewish, the leper was ostracized from society as a person who had been supernaturally plagued because of wrongdoing. This separation is nowhere more evident than in the Dead Sea Scrolls. The leper is given a special shelter outside both sacred and ordinary cities. He is not allowed to mingle with other persons, except perhaps other lepers. Eating the pure, communal food of the sect is out of the question. In order to eat even ordinary food, the leper must first immerse in water.

Several of the Cave 4 fragments of the Damascus Document discuss *ṣaraʿat* in terms of punishment for sin. Like the Rabbis, the author considers a leper to be a sinner on whom God has sent a plague (cf. t. *Neg.* 6.7; b. *Ber.* 5b). 4Q270 lists the leper in a catalogue of transgressors. The author explicitly connects leprosy and sin by attributing the disease to an evil spirit which interferes with the flow of blood: '... the sp[irit] enters [and takes] hold of the artery, (making) the blood [recede up]wards and downwards ...' (4Q266 2–3). Another fragment of the Damascus Document describes leprosy as an evil spirit which enters the body (4Q267 9 i). Some fragments state that *ṣaraʿat* is not only induced by a spirit but is healed when the spirit of life returns (4Q268; 4Q272).

Several other scrolls concur with the Damascus Document that leprosy comes because of sin. The Hodayot praise God for the healing of leprosy, 'You have strengthened the spirit of a man in front of a plague [of scale disease] and have purified the life of your servant from a multitude of sins' (1QH 1.32) (cf. Qimron 1991: 256–59). Also 4Q512 28 viii, describes a purifying leper as a repentant sinner. At the time of his purification, the leper confesses, 'I have sinned' (Baillet 1982: 262–86). MMT lists the leper's sins as slander and blasphemy (MMT B 73).

Leprosy is considered a divine curse throughout the ancient world and is of particular concern in the Bible (Milgrom 1991: 820–21). According to Leviticus, the purifying leper must bring several atoning sacrifices in order to be purified of this impurity (Lev. 14.19-20). Furthermore, Scripture records several examples of leprosy used as a punishment from God: Miriam was punished with leprosy and did not recover until Moses prayed for her healing (Num. 12.9-11). God threatened the Israelites that if they disobeyed him he would smite them with boils, scabs and itches (Deut. 28.27; cf. Lev. 26.21). He also threatened to damage their houses with leprosy (Lev. 14.34). Isaiah warned the women of Jerusalem that God would inflict scabs on their heads because of their vanity (Isa. 3.17). King Uzziah broke out with leprosy on his forehead when he presumed to offer incense in the sanctuary, a function restricted to priests alone (2 Chron. 26.23). Job's friends assumed that God had smitten Job with leprosy since his skin had erupted with boils (Job 22.5; cf. 11.6). Only Yahweh's prophet could intervene for Naaman, the Syrian general, who had contracted leprosy. Sometimes a righteous person curses someone with leprosy, and God honours that pronouncement. For example, David effectively cursed Joab's line so that it always included a leper (2 Sam. 3.29) and Elisha transferred Naaman's leprosy to Gehazi, the prophet's greedy servant (2 Kgs 5.27).

The Dead Sea Scroll authors are not the only group who continue the notion that leprosy comes because of sin. The Rabbis connect the affliction with gossip and arrogance (t. *Neg.* 6.7) because these sins brought leprosy to Miriam and Uzziah, respectively, in Scripture (*Sif. meṣ. neg. par.* 5.7-9).

As evident from the above data, the ancient Jewish concern with leprosy is not primarily a matter of physical health. How to heal a person from leprosy is a closed question. The matter is left up to God who can bestow or withhold healing. The interest of the Torah, the Scrolls and the Rabbis is on proper purification after God has granted mercy, forgiven the sin and healed the disease.

The claim of several scholars that the life–death principle undergirds the biblical impurity system (see Chapter 1) is supported at Qumran, especially in the case of the leper. Many aspects of corpse impurity apply to leprosy as well: (1) the leper's dishevelled hair and rent clothes can be a sign that 'the leper may be mourning his own "death"' (Frymer-Kensky 1983: 400); (2) the living bird which is dipped in the blood of the dead bird and then freed is symbolic and brings to mind the plight of the leper himself who has just been 'set free from his brush with death' (ibid.); (3)

the use of hyssop, cedarwood and crimson wool in both the red cow rite and the purification of the leper emphasizes redness and points to blood, the purgative element in both rites; (4) both the leper and the corpse contaminate people by a shared overhang; (5) both the leper and the corpse must be isolated from the community; (6) sacrifices are necessary in both cases: for the corpse-impure the red cow must be sacrificed; for the leper, four sacrifices are brought at the completion of purification; and (7) the purification of leper and the leprous house, like the corpse-impure person, involves a seven-day process (cf. also Harrington 1993: 202, for Rabbinic parallels between leprosy and death).

In addition to these correlations between corpse impurity and leprosy, the Scrolls make the connection between the two explicit. According to the sect, the leper's uncleanness is due to blockage of the 'spirit of life'. Thus, the leper, the most contaminating of all living impurity bearers, can be considered an oxymoron, 'a living corpse' barred from participation in communal worship of the living God of Israel.

Further Reading

Baumgarten, J.M.

1996 *Qumran Cave Four XIII: The Damascus Document (4Q266–273), Discoveries in the Judaean Desert XVIII* (Oxford: Clarendon Press).

Milgrom, J.

1991 *Leviticus 1–16*, The Anchor Bible 3A (Garden City, NY: Doubleday).

1994b '4QTOHOROT[a]: An Unpublished Qumran Text on Parities', in *Time to Prepare the Way in the Wilderness: Papers on the Qumran Scrolls*, eds. D. Dimant and L.H. Schiffman (Leiden: E.J. Brill): 59–68.

Qimron, E.

1991 'Notes on the 4Q Zadokite Fragment on Skin Disease', *JJS* 42/2: 256–59.

Rabinowitz, L.I.

1971 'Leprosy', in *Encyclopedia Judaica*, XI (Jerusalem: Keter): 33–39.

Wilkinson, J.

1977 'Leprosy and Leviticus: The Problem of Description and Identification', *Scot J Th* 30: 153–69.

5

BODILY DISCHARGES

1. Introduction

Discharges from the body are a major source of impurity in ancient Judaism. From Scripture to the Talmud, Jewish sages and priests have carefully prescribed ways of dealing with sexual flows and the elimination of body waste. Women were sometimes secluded during their menstrual periods or, as in the Qumran group, excluded altogether. Abnormal sexual flows, whether male or female, were looked upon as dangerous and even as punishment from God. Since ritual impurity was contagious, persons emitting discharges were expected to avoid unwanted contact with other people.

Restrictions which regulate social as well as physical intercourse between pure individuals and those with flows abound in the literature. An example outside of the Qumran corpus illustrates the level of concern. Not only did pure individuals separate themselves from those known to be impure but, according to the Mishnah, a man already suffering from an abnormal sexual discharge should also not eat with his menstruating wife (m. *Shab*. 1.3; cf. Baumgarten 1999b: 79). Even though both individuals were already impure, the Sages were concerned that further impurity might result between them and so ruled a separation of the two.

Below is a discussion of the available information of the Scrolls on the impurity of bodily discharges. The data is organized by impurity type: abnormal flow (male), abnormal flow (female), childbirth, menstruation, semen, and excrement. In each case the important questions have to do with exclusion, contamination and purification, i.e. how severe was the separation or exclusion of the impure person? What was the extent of contamination? What was the prescribed mode of purification? A final section looks at the significance of the data and examines why discharges were deemed to cause so much ritual impurity.

2. Abnormal Flow (Male)

The *zab* is a man who has an abnormal sexual discharge. Abnormal flux, or flow, is usually equated with gonorrhea but can refer to any abnormal, urethral secretion (Milgrom 1991: 907). This kind of flow is not the result of ejaculation; the fluid simply oozes out. The *zab* is discussed in the Temple Scroll and in a number of fragments from Cave 4.

Several texts imply that the *zab* and other impure persons must be isolated from the community, even from other types of impure persons (4Q274 1.1-5; 11Q19 46.17-18). 4QTohorot, fragment 1, begins with a proscription probably intended for the *zab*, since the author focuses on the contamination of the bed and seat, the text continuing with proscriptions for the menstruant and the *zabah*, following the same order as Leviticus 15 (Baumgarten 1999b: 101–102). The Qumran author stipulates that the impure person keep a distance of 18 feet away from the communal, pure food and 18 feet north-west of any dwelling (4Q274 1.2-3). Those afflicted with the disease are in a perpetual state of mourning: 'He shall begin to lay his pl[ea]. He shall lie in a [b]ed of sorrow and reside in [a dwelling of] sighs' (4Q274 1). The Temple Scroll places the *zab* 'to the east of the city' (11Q19 46.17). Both the Scrolls and the Talmud derive this ostracization from the biblical injunction on the leper: 'Alone shall he dwell' (Lev. 13.46; b. *Pes.* 67a). Nevertheless, although the Rabbis banish the leper from the city, they exclude the *zab* only from the Temple Mount (m. *Kel.* 1.3; m. *Zab.* 5.6-7).

Anything the *zab* touches becomes impure and contaminating to other persons, according to 4QTohorot. 4Q274 1 i 4-5 reads: 'As for the woman who is discharging blood, for seven days she shall not touch a male with a genital flux, or any object [th]at he has either touched, l[ain] upon, or sat on. [And if] she has touched, she shall launder her clothes, bathe, and afterwards she may eat' (tr. Milgrom). According to Scripture, the *zab*'s bed and chair will contaminate those who touch them because the *zab* has lain or sat on them, but objects he has merely touched do not become contaminants (Lev. 15.5-6).

4Q274 also reveals that any impure person who touches the *zab* receives added impurity and must bathe (*raḫaṣ ba-mayim*) and launder before eating. A menstruant may not touch a *zab* (during her impure week) nor anything (*keli*) the *zab* has touched or lain on (4Q274 1 i 4-5). If she does, she must launder her clothes and bathe (*raḫaṣ*), and then she may eat. The writer supports this with Lev. 14, 'Impure, impure shall he call out', claiming that the correct rendering is 'impure to the impure' (cf. also *Targ. Ps.-Jon.* on Lev. 13–14).

In the area of contamination it is instructive to note the comparative lenience of Rabbinic law. According to the Mishnah, (1) not everything under the *zab* is so impure as to contaminate those sitting/lying on it – only his bed, chair and saddle; (2) not every object the *zab* touches is contaminated – only susceptible items (primarily, usable vessels made of wood, clay, fabric, skin) and these are not contaminating to other persons; (3) the *zab* is not expelled from Jerusalem or any other city; and (4) there is no increase of impurity for those already impure.

According to Leviticus, the *zab* who touches a pure person *without first washing his hands* defiles the pure individual (Lev. 15.11). Thus, if the *zab* did wash his hands, his touch would not defile. Tohorot supports the effectiveness of the *zab*'s handwashing: 'And anyone touched by [a man who has] a flux [ ] [and whose] hand[s were not] r[in]sed in water becomes [impure]' (4Q277 1 i 10-11).

The *zab* who has been healed and is now undergoing purification is in an intermediate state of pollution. Fragment 4Q274 seems to imply that he may touch pure individuals without rendering them impure, 'And the one who is counting (*sofer*), male or female, must not touch a *zab* or a menstruant, *unless she has been purified*; for the blood of menstruation is like the flux and the one touching it ...' (4Q274 1 i 7-8). From the italicized phrase we might infer that if a purifying *zab* touched a pure woman, she would remain pure. But this contradicts the plain meaning of Scripture which states that the purifying *zab* does not become pure until the end of the seventh day and is not allowed access to holy things until the eighth day when he brings atoning sacrifices (Lev. 15.13-15). Also, 4Q274 2 i 3 states that a person purifying from corpse contamination may not touch any pure item until the sprinkling of *me niddah* on the seventh day; so also 11Q19 49.20-21. Thus, 4Q274 1 i 7 must be arguing that the purifying person who touches a menstruant becomes more impure just as if the purifying person had touched a *zab*, the point being, as the text continues, that flux and menses contaminate equally and that an already impure person (in this case, a purifying person) can contract additional impurity.

The chart below (Table 2) organizes the information on impurity contagion of the *zab* from the Tohorot texts. Since Tohorot regards flux, menstruation and semen at the same level of contagion (4Q274 1.8), the chart reads '*zab*' for a person with any kind of discharge.[1]

1. I follow J. Baumgarten's reading of line 8: '... And when [a man has] an emiss[ion] of semen his touch is defiling ...' 1999: 103, and see discussion there.

Table 2

ZAB	CONTACT	RESULT
Zab 4Q274 1 i 3	touches impure person	impure person (probably including *zab*) must bathe and launder
Zab 4Q274 1 i 5	touches pure person	pure person becomes impure
Zab with washed hands Lev. 15.11	touches pure person	no impurity transmitted
Purifying *zab* 4Q274 1 i 8	touches impure person	purifying *zab* must bathe and launder
Purifying *zab* cf. Lev. 15.13; 4Q274 2 i 3; 11Q19 49.20-21	touches pure person	pure person becomes impure
Objects touched by a *zab* 4Q274 1 i 4	which are touched by anyone (pure or impure)	person who touches object must purify

Purification of the *zab* is outlined in Scripture and confirmed by the Temple Scroll. According to the Torah, the *zab* remains outside the city until he is healed (Num. 5.2). He then counts seven days and, if no discharge appears, he immerses completely in running water and launders his clothes on the seventh day. 4Q512 gives a fragmentary description of the *zab*'s purification blessing, '[And when] the seven days of his pur[ification have been completed . . .] he will purify his clothes with water [and wash his body . . .] And he will cover himself with his clothes and bless on [. . .] God of Israel [. . .]' (4Q512 10–11 x, tr. F. García Martínez). With typical Qumran modesty, the purifying *zab* puts on his clothes before he prays. The purifying *zab* is now ritually pure for all contacts within the profane sphere. According to the Temple Scroll, he may now enter the Temple City (11Q19 45.15-17).

On the eighth day, the purifying *zab* comes to the Temple to offer the sacrifices which will conclude his purification and give him the access of a layperson to sancta (Lev. 15.14). The Temple Scroll does not regard the *zab* as completely purified until sunset on the eighth day (11Q19 45.15-17). This contrasts with the Rabbinic assertion that the offerings of the eighth day conclude the *zab*'s purification.

Some scholars suggest that bodily flows were cleansed by the sprinkling of *me niddah*, the special purgation water used to purify corpse impurity (see Chapter 3). Some point to 4Q512 which states that purgation water is used for those 'impure for many days'. According to this view, in addition to the *zab*'s immersion and laundering, he would also be sprinkled by the priest with *me niddah*. Indeed, Tohorot does compare the contagion of the *zab* to that of a corpse (4Q274 1 i 9).[2]

Purifying persons, as mentioned earlier, pose a particular threat in terms of contamination of food, because they are not sequestered away from the community like impure persons but come within the camp in order to undergo purification. Therefore, during purification individuals must be careful to avoid susceptible, pure persons and items, otherwise they will contaminate them. They must also avoid impure persons, lest they contract further impurity.

3. Abnormal Flow (Female)

The *zabah* is the female counterpart of the *zab*, a woman with an abnormal discharge of blood. Both 4Q274 and Scripture refer to a woman with a flow of blood lasting many days (4Q274 1 i 66; Lev. 15.25). This discharge would occur outside of or extend beyond the woman's week of menstrual impurity. An example of such a woman may be the desperate woman described in the Gospels who had endured a haemorrhage for 12 years before she fearfully approached Jesus for healing (Mk 5.25-27); by revealing her condition she would also be warning him of ritual contamination if he were to touch her. The laws of Leviticus 15.1-15 regarding contamination and purification of the *zab* appear to apply also to the *zabah* (Milgrom 1991: 947–48; see Table 2 above for the contamination and purification of the *zab*).

The laws of the *zabah* provide a fine opportunity for comparison of the exegetical methods of the Qumran authors vis-à-vis the Rabbis. Lev. 15.25 states that the abnormal discharge lasts a vague 'many days'. The Rabbis interpret this to mean at least three successive days of abnormal bleeding (*Sif. meṣ. zab. par.* 5.9). The sectarians seem to focus on the rest of the verse, 'if it run beyond the time of her menstruation all the days of the

2. Corpse impurity is juxtaposed with *zab* and other impurities in 4Q277. Touching the bed of a *zab* is further compared to corpse impurity in 4Q278, cf. Baumgarten 1999b: 118. E. Eshel follows Baumgarten in her comments on 4Q414 and 4Q512, 1999: 139. Nevertheless, the corpse's overhang contagion is nowhere applied to the *zab*.

issue of her impurity shall be as the days of her menstruation: she shall be impure'. They read the verse more stringently and define the *zabah* as a woman who discharges any amount of blood outside of the seven-day menstrual period (4Q267 9 ii 2-4).

According to the Temple Scroll, areas are to be allocated within ordinary cities for those with sexual discharges (11Q19 48.15-16), and they are not allowed at all in the Temple City. The purifying *zabah*, who has been healed and is going through purification, like the purifying *zab*, is probably allowed access to the ordinary city if she first bathes and launders (4Q514 5–6). The Scroll authors, like the Rabbis, assume that all of the purification procedures of the *zab* apply to the *zabah*, including sacrifices and ablutions. According to the Damascus Document, the *zabah* is not considered totally pure until sunset on the eighth day (4Q267 9 ii 4).

4. Childbirth

According to Scripture, two periods of impurity apply to the parturient (the woman who has just given birth). The parturient is impure for a week if birthing a boy, two weeks for a girl (4Q267 9 ii 5; Lev. 12.2-3). She remains at a lesser stage of impurity for 33 more days if the child is a boy and 66 days of lesser impurity if the child is a girl. According to the Rabbis, the difference in the two stages is that in the first, more severe stage, she is prohibited from contact with food, persons and cooking utensils, lest she contaminate them. In the second stage, she is clean for all activities within the lay sphere but cannot enter sacred space, i.e. she may not go to the Temple or handle holy food gifts (Lev. 12.4). The Damascus Document suggests that even during the lesser impurity period the mother conveys impurity. She apparently would convey impurity to her newborn, since the text speaks of a 'wet nurse' for the child (4Q266 6 ii 11).

The greater length of the parturient's impurity in the case of a baby girl has been much debated. According to R. Simeon b. Yohai, the first stages of impurity (seven days if the child is male; fourteen days if female) were originally the same length (two weeks) but in the case of the boy the time was reduced so that circumcision could take place in a state of purity on the eighth day (Milgrom 1991). It seems more likely that the authors simply regard the baby girl as a greater impurity threat than the boy, since she will generate more impurity throughout the course of her life due to her monthly menstrual period and her times of childbirth.

4Q Miscellaneous Rules, 4Q265, mentions the impurity rules of the parturient. Joseph Baumgarten masterfully uses *Jubilees* to restore blanks in 4Q265, lines 11-13. Adam does not come into the Garden of Eden immediately and neither does Eve. They probably wait 40 and 80 days, respectively, taking into account the impurity of childbirth. The new couple do not partake of any holy thing until after this period (Cf. *Jub.* 3.12; 1QH[a] 16.10-13; Life of Adam; Lk. 2.22). It seems that a principle found often in the Qumran texts is surfacing here as well: humanity is born in an impure condition, coming into the world brings impurity (even for Adam and Eve) (cf. 1QH 9.22; 1QS 9.9-10).

According to the Temple Scroll, a pregnant woman who miscarries becomes impure like a grave as long as the dead foetus remains within her (11Q19 50.10-11) (See pp. 74–75 for discussion.). The notion that the pregnant woman can become a 'tomb' is unique to Qumran.

The impurity of the parturient is a cross-cultural phenomenon. At Delos 'neither births nor deaths were permitted to occur there' (Thucydides 3.04). According to Cyrene law the parturient contaminates for three days all who come under her roof. Even the two stages of impurity are attested elsewhere. The Hittites observed a longer period of impurity after the birth of a girl than a boy (four months vs. three months). A similar difference applies today in Northern India, although in Southern India the longer impurity period applies if the child is a boy (Maccoby 1999: 49).

5. Menstruation

Menstrual impurity was a major concern among the Scroll authors. Even though Qumran appears to be a community of celibate men, they interpreted the law as it should apply to Jews everywhere. Indeed they expected the Messiah to one day lead them out of their self-imposed exile and re-establish the nation according to the correct interpretation of the Torah. Also, some of the documents of the sect reflect different periods in its history. For example, the Damascus Document appears to be a parent document which is older than the migration to Qumran.

The Admonition of the Damascus Document rebukes priests for having sexual intercourse with menstruants and polluting the sanctuary (CD 5.7; cf. 4Q266 6 ii 2). Sleeping with menstruants was labelled 'a net of Belial' because it was not just a matter of ritual impurity but a direct violation of the law (Lev. 15.24; cf. also Ezek. 18.6). 4Q266 6 ii 2 reads, 'One who has sexual intercourse with her [a menstruant] will bear the [s]in of her impurity on him and be impure seven days.' The violator incurs the *karet* penalty, i.e. 'calamity to his entire lineage through the direct intervention of God ... and without necessitating social action' (cf. Lev. 18.29; Frymer-Kensky 1983: 405).

The definition and derivation of the term *niddah* is instructive. According to Moshe Greenberg, the best morphological explanation is that the term derives from the root NDD meaning 'distancing', both in a physical sense (i.e. flight from) and in an emotional sense (i.e. recoil, abhorrence) (Greenberg 1995: 69). J. Milgrom concurs and suggests the following translation for *niddah*, 'expulsion, elimination', i.e. discharge of menstrual blood, which came to mean, on the one hand, menstrual impurity (and impurity in general), and on the other the menstruant herself, excluded from society' (Milgrom 1991: 745). NDD has a close connection with NDH, which simply indicates separation. The basic sense of *niddah*, then, has to do with distancing and separation; not only the discharge of the blood flow, but also the separation of women from normal social contacts during their menstrual period (Greenberg 1995: 74–75; Milgrom 1991: 745, 948–50; Meacham 1999: 23–39).

In Qumran legal texts the term *niddah* refers to the state of menstrual impurity, but in non-legal texts it usually refers to impurity in a general sense (Greenberg 1995: 75; Licht 1965b: 96; Yadin 1983: 192–93; Nitzan 1986: 90–91). When referring to the menstruant herself the authors prefer the more euphemistic term *davah*, 'woman with a flow'. In mishnaic Hebrew, *davah* is replaced by *niddah*, which no longer denotes a state of impurity but the menstruant herself.

Qumran texts exclude the menstruant from society. The Temple Scroll, for example, provides no structures for women during their impurity, although it does provide them for other impure persons. As Yadin said, from the lack of these structures and the fact that sexual intercourse was not allowed in the city, women were probably not allowed to live there (Yadin 1983: 306). According to the Temple Scroll, menstruants are allowed to remain in ordinary cities but must be quarantined: '... Among your cities you shall establish a place ... for those who have gonorrhea and for women when they are in their unclean menstruation and after giving birth, so that they do not defile in their midst with their unclean menstruation ...' (11Q19 48.13-17). The notion that women should be isolated during their menstrual impurity may also be present in the records of Josephus and the Rabbis (*Ant.* 3.261; m. *Nid.* 7.4; *Targ. Ps.-Jon.* on Lev. 12.2; *ARN A* 2.3).

According to 4Q265 and the Temple Scroll no woman was allowed to eat of the Passover sacrifice, although it seems that eating the passover as a family was common practice in Jerusalem (4Q265 3; 11Q19 17.8-9; *War* 6.426; m. *Pes.* 8.1). The concern of the Qumran authors is that the Passover sacrifice will become defiled. In fact, men were not allowed to share their portions of the Passover with their families, considering it a 'breach of trust' against the other members of the community. As J. Baumgarten explains, 'For by involving those whose ritual purity was in doubt, the errant partner was seen as subverting the purity of the common meal' (Baumgarten 1999b: 64). Clearly, according to these Scroll authors, women obstructed the maintenance of holiness.

Ancient texts from other groups, Jewish and non-Jewish, indicate that the separation of the menstruant was a cross-cultural phenomenon. In Hellenistic times the menstruant, and often women in general, were derided. According to Aristotle, the menstruant dimmed a mirror in front of her and a parturient, according to Cyrene law, conveyed a three-day contamination to everyone in the house with her (Parker 1983: 78, 102–103, 336). Superstitions surface in the Talmud as well: according to one text, the breath of the menstruant is dangerous and if she walks between two men, one will die (b. *Pes.* 111a). The later *Baraita de Massekhet Niddah* states that the dust of a *niddah*'s feet causes impurity to others, she makes food and utensils impure and she may not go to the synagogue or make Sabbath blessings (Meacham 1999: 32).

The disposal of blood is of primary importance in biblical tradition. Menstrual blood is a potent contaminant in the system of ritual impurity and innocent bloodshed is the primary pollutant of the land (Frymer-Kensky 1983: 401). At Qumran the contamination of the menstruant is discussed in a few fragmentary texts. Tohorot warns her not to mingle with other people during her week of impurity so as not to contaminate (*tig'al*) the 'camps of the holy ones of Israel' (4Q274 1 i 4-6). She must not touch *zabim* either or anything they have touched or lain on. If she does, she must launder her clothes and bathe (*rahas*), and then she may eat.

Tohorot regards menstrual blood at the same contamination level as the flow of the *zab* and *zabah*, '... for the blood of menstruation is like the flux and the one touching it ...' (4Q274 1 i 7-8). This is an indication of the Qumran authors' homogenization tendency, i.e. raising the level of restrictions to apply equally to all members of a particular category (see Chapter 1). This parity of blood and flux probably applies only to the contamination power of the discharge and does not mean that all of the restrictions regarding *zabim* apply as well to menstruants. Scripture's rules regarding *zabim* are much stricter than those applying to the menstruant. The Torah banishes *zabim* from the camp (Num. 5.2). Their week of purification does not begin until their flux ceases and they must bring sacrifices at the end of that week (Lev. 15.29). By contrast, the menstruant is not banished by Scripture and her week of purification begins with her first bleeding (Lev. 15.19).

In later times, the Rabbis treat the menstruant as a *zabah* in the sense that her purificatory week does not begin until she has stopped bleeding. Apparently, the problem was that women had trouble in keeping track of their menstrual cycle, which often changed from month to month, and there was a fear that sexual intercourse might occur during bleeding, a clear violation of Scripture (Cohen 1999: 44–45). However, the Rabbinic rule resulted in a difficult compromise: a twelve-day purification period, five days for actual menstruation and then a week of 'whitening' or clean days. No sexual intercourse was allowed during the entire period.

Like all other temporarily impure persons, a menstruant must immerse in water and launder her clothes, at least according to one Qumran author (4Q514 5–6). Some scholars have suggested that the Torah does not require bathing for menstruants because it is not explicitly stated in Leviticus 15. Others have said that water was scarce and, the menstruant's condition being habitual, there would have been insufficient water to accommodate all women after their monthly impurity. Still others point to the traditions of the Karaites who simply sprinkled menstruants with water for purification (Cohen 1999: 92–93; Meacham 1999: 28). Nevertheless, the Qumran author follows the most logical reading of Leviticus 15, where bathing is an implied requirement after menstruation since even those who touch the menstruant must bathe (Lev. 15.19). The Rabbis too make this connection and require the menstruant to bathe (m. *Miq*. 8.1, 5).

6. Semen

The group who made their home at Qumran was apparently celibate (see above under 'Menstruation'). The foundational texts of the community promote abstinence in order to create a 'holy house for Aaron'. Josephus confirms celibacy for a group of the Essenes and, writing for a Hellenistic audience, attributes it to a desire to master passion as well as to a negative  view of women as quarrelsome and lascivious (*Ant*. 18.21; *War* 2.120-21). But there is more to the Qumran rejection of women than this. The Scrolls demonstrate that the sectarians wanted to maintain holiness at a very high level, avoiding impurity whenever possible. Certainly this, in large part, is the reason they abstained from conjugal relations.

Some scrolls prohibit sexual intercourse in the holy city, Jerusalem, the 'City of the Temple' (CD 12.1-2). According to the Temple Scroll, the man discharging semen is put outside of the Temple City for three days and quarantined within ordinary cities (11Q19 46.16-18; 48.13-17). The author requires men who have had a seminal emission within the holy city to leave until they are purified. He seems to be following the model of the three-day encampment at Sinai, where, in preparation for the holy encounter with God, marital relations were not allowed (Yadin 1983: 135). As another holy encampment, the Temple City could not be defiled by sexual relations either. The Temple Scroll author apparently prohibits women to reside in the Temple City since no quarters are provided for them during times of impurity as they are for other impure persons. In reality, women do not appear to be restricted in Second Temple Jerusalem except at the sanctuary itself, where a Court of the Women was established in the time of Herod.

Women are excluded from other holy areas, at least in part on the basis of impurity. The Rule of the Congregation excludes the impure and disabled and women from participation in the messianic community (1Q28a 2.5), and the War Scroll excludes them from the War Camp (1QM 7.4-6). The Qumran Community was considered a temporary substitute for the Temple by its members, and this 'house of holiness' would certainly be compromised by sexual relations.

In other cities, sexual intercourse was apparently allowed only for procreation and hence no sexual intercourse was allowed during pregnancy, probably because no child could result from it.[3] Also, the text forbids '*zenut* with one's wife', which is somewhat unclear but probably prohibits intercourse for pleasure only, rather than for procreation (4Q269 12.4-5; 4Q270 7 i 13; cf. *War* 2.120). A second wife, even for the ruler, was, according to the Temple Scroll, out of the question unless the first wife dies (11Q19 57.17-19).

The Qumran sect realized that its rejection of marriage was not the norm for Jewish life, nor was it a biblical mandate. The Damascus Document, which has been attested at Qumran, clarifies the difference. Those who live as celibates are *ʿanshe tamim qodesh* – 'men of perfect holiness', but those who choose family life are *ka-serekh ha-ʿares*, 'according to the way of the land' (CD 7.4-7; cf. *War* 2.160). Nevertheless, the man striving for perfect holiness will be celibate.

Tohorot regards semen as more defiling than a straightforward reading of Scripture would suggest. Leviticus prescribes purification for those in contact with semen directly but not for those who touch the man who has emitted the semen (Lev. 15.17). According to Tohorot, individuals who handle anything which has been in contact with semen either directly or indirectly, e.g. by carrying a contaminated garment without direct contact on top of a pile of clean clothes, become impure and must launder their

3. Baumgarten 1995a: 448 also suggests that it might be due to 'fear that coital pressure during pregnancy might lead to bleeding, thus making intercourse illicit'.

clothes (4Q274 2 i 8). This is commensurate with the added stringency regarding semen reflected in the Temple Scroll, which denies entrance to the Temple City for three days to both *zabim* and those who have had a seminal emission (11Q19 45.11-12).

Semen impurity is more severe at Qumran than among the Rabbis. For the latter, the bed and seat of those who have discharged semen do not have the potency to defile other persons and objects. Also, according to the Mishnah, semen does not defile except by direct contact (b. *Naz.* 66a; m. *Zab.* 5.11; *Sif. meṣ. zab.* 2.8). *Midras,* or pressure without direct contact, does apply to gonorrhea but not to semen. The Rabbis make a distinction between normal and abnormal body discharges.

Purification of someone with semen impurity is more stringent, according to the Temple Scroll, if that person is trying to enter the holy city. Those who are approaching the city but have had sexual intercourse must bathe and launder and remain outside in a special area for three days, and before they enter the city they must bathe and launder again (11Q19 45.11-12; cf. CD 12.1-2). By contrast, the Rabbis consider such persons pure for all ordinary purposes immediately after immersion, and for all sacred purposes after the next sunset (m. *TY* 2.2-3; *Sif. shem. sher.* 8.9). If a man is already in the Temple City and has a nocturnal emission, he may not enter the Temple until three days have passed (11Q19 45.7-8). He must bathe and launder his clothes on the first and third days; he is pure at sunset. J. Baumgarten has suggested that semen impurity, like corpse impurity, may even require the use of purgation water.[4]

4Q274 brings up a case where a man owns only one set of clothes. If the clothes did not directly come into contact with the semen, e.g. the man merely touched someone with semen impurity, he is permitted to wear his clothes without laundering them. Nevertheless, he must make sure his clothes do not come into contact with the food he eats. In order to avoid undue hardship, the text allows the needy person to eat ordinary food, but not sacred food, before completing his laundry (4Q274 2 i 6-9). At first glance this seems like a concession for the needy, but when compared with Rabbinic halakha it is not such a leniency. The idea that a person must bathe and launder simply because he touched an individual with semen impurity is not in Rabbinic halakha; indirect contact with

4. Baumgarten (1999b: 83–87, 104), refers to 4Q284, fragment 1, on the festal calendar, a text which mentions 'purgation water', *me niddah,* and 'semen'. He suggests that the group may have required the stronger purification of *me niddah* for purification from semen and all other impurities. Another possible interpretation is that at festivals the sect required purification with *me niddah* to neutralize any possible corpse or carcass impurity a person may have contracted unwittingly.

semen does not contaminate individuals (b. *Naz.* 66a; cf. m. *Zab.* 5.11; *Sif. meṣ. zab.* 2.8 – the notion of *midras* does not apply to semen impurity).

Thus, the Qumran sectarians hold a more stringent stance toward semen impurity than found in Rabbinic halakha: (1) no provision is made for a *tebul yom*; the man impure from semen must wait until his purification is complete with the setting of the sun. The Rabbis, by contrast, allow the man full freedom to move about in society immediately after bathing, as long as he does not come into contact with sancta. (2) Indirect contact with semen, e.g. touching a person who has emitted semen or touching his clothes or bed (but not the semen itself), according to these Qumran fragments, causes impurity. The Rabbis limit this secondary defilement only to food, liquids and hands. And (3) the three-day purification required for semen impurity before entry into the Temple City and the possible sprinkling of the individual with purgation water represent a marked stringency, since Rabbinic halakha requires only a one-day purification and reserves purgation water for the corpse-impure.

7. Excrement

The impurity of excrement is noted in very few places in the Qumran Scrolls. The Temple Scroll requires latrines to be set up north-east of the Temple City; these are houses with pits in them for excrement. They are at least 4500 feet away from the city boundary. The idealism of the Temple Scroll is revealed when one realizes that the author limits walking on the Sabbath to about 3500 feet (11Q19 46.15; cf. 4Q265 7 i 3). This in effect prohibits defecation on the Sabbath. Other Qumran texts emphasize the need for purity on the Sabbath and other holy days (cf. 4Q251; 4Q274 2 i) and 4Q265 explicitly forbids wearing garments soiled with excrement on the Sabbath (4Q265 6.2).

In 4Q472a, a small fragment of text, the words *mikhse so* can be detected. If one takes *so* as an abbreviated form of *so'ah*, the meaning would be 'covering excrement' (Geiger 1928: 264; Baumgarten 1999b: 156). Josephus refers to a section along Jerusalem's western wall as *Bethso*, a term Y. Yadin rendered as *Beit So'ah*, latrine (Yadin 1983: 303). The Essene Gate possibly led to this latrine. 4Q472a also mentions a *shalish*, which may be a hollowed hatchet used for covering excrement (Baumgarten 1999b: 156). R. de Vaux found an iron tool in Cave 11, which he suggested may represent this type of hatchet. Isa. 40.12 uses *shalish* as a vessel or measure of capacity in which earth is collected. Also, archaeologists have tentatively identified a cesspit on the east side of the site at Qumran, next to a pool for purification (Magness 2000: 718).

The above data fits with Josephus' description of the Essenes. He states that the Essenes buried and covered excrement so as not to offend the deity. In his description of Essene Sabbath restrictions he states:

> ...They are stricter than any other of the Jews in resting from their labors on the seventh day; for they not only get their food ready the day before, that they may not be obliged to kindle a fire on that day, but they will not remove any vessel out of its place, nor go to stool thereon. Nay, on the other days they dig a small pit, a foot deep, with a paddle (which kind of hatchet is given them when they are first admitted among them); and covering themselves round with their garment, that they may not affront the divine rays of light, they ease themselves into that pit, after which they put the earth that was dug out again in to the pit; and even this they do only in the more lonely places, which they choose out for this purpose, and although this easement of the body be natural, yet it is a rule with them to wash themselves after it, as if it were a defilement to them. (*War* 2.147–49)

The Torah does not include excrement in its discussion of ritual impurities (Lev. 11–15; Num. 19). There is a mention of it in Deuteronomy which prohibits defecation in the war camp (Deut. 23.13-15). Soldiers must take a stick and bury their excrement outside the camp. However, no purification, e.g bathing and/or laundering, is prescribed. The language of ritual purity is not used, although it is God's holiness that is offended by defecation within the War Camp. Ezekiel, on the other hand, recoils at God's request to use human excrement as fuel for cooking food (Ezek. 4.10-15). The prophet protests that he has never defiled himself with forbidden food. This passage may have been an influence on the Dead Sea sectarians since it links excrement with impurity (Milgrom 1991: 536).

The notion that excrement causes ritual impurity contrasts sharply with the view of the Mishnah and other Rabbinic literature. According to the Jerusalem Talmud, excrement does not defile (y. *Pes.* 7.11). The Rabbis refer the Deuteronomy 23 restriction on excrement only to the sanctuary itself. The Temple is analogous to the War Camp. Temple lavatories are described next to the ritual pool which is located below the courts and reached by a tunnel (m. *Tam.* 1.1).

Rabbinic statements about excrement consistently occur in discussions of *neqiyyut*, physical cleanliness, rather than *tohorah*, ritual purity. For example, 'Rabbi Yose said: Is excrement impurity [*tum'ah*]? Why, it is nothing but cleanliness [*neqiyyut*]' (y. *Pes.* 7.12). Excrement is said to cleanse the body, as in the statement that saintly persons evacuate their bowels shortly before death so that they can come into the

Divine Presence in the resurrection in a seemly state (b. *Shab.* 118b; *Gen. R.* 82).

In other cultures, excrement is sometimes considered ritually defiling as well as a matter of physical impurity. The distinction between the two is often blurred. Human faeces are impure in Hinduism (Manu 5.138ff) and in Iranian religion (Vend. 17.11ff) (Maccoby 1999: 66 n 4).

8. Significance

It has been said that death and sexual processes are what make human beings mortal (Wright 1992: 729–41). In ancient Judaism it is precisely the life–death cycle, from conception and birth to death, which generates impurity. As Leslie Cook says, ritual purity 'centers around sexual differentiation, involuntary seminal emissions, disease, and death because it is these issues of corporeality that, in the Bible, symbolize the difference between human beings and God' (Cook 1999: 49). Acknowledging this difference between humanity and deity by keeping mortality and its impurity away from the sacred realm is essential for the continued welfare of Israel. As Jacob Milgrom says: 'Because the quintessential source of holiness resides with God, Israel is enjoined to control the occurrence of impurity lest it impinge on his realm' (Milgrom 1991: 47).

Mary Douglas suggests that a society's restrictions on the human body reflect its efforts to regulate the social body, the community. Minority groups suffering persecution tend to impose strict rules on the body, regulating everything which comes in or goes out of it. These rules on the physical body mirror the strict regulations on the social body which too is concerned about maintaining its boundaries and filtering all unwanted elements (Douglas 1966: 124; 1975: 269). This general explanation does fit, by and large, with the stringent laws on bodily discharges that one finds among the sectarians of Qumran.

Sexual flows, menstruation and seminal discharges are all either life-giving or life-diminishing body fluids. They not only give human beings life but remind them of the certainty of death. On the one hand, through sexual relations a human being becomes a participant in the very creation of human life. On the other hand, in the discharge of sexual fluids individuals are reminded of their physical mortality as they lose life-giving forces (Milgrom 1989b: 103–109).

The parturient is at the very threshold of life and death. Indeed the number of women who died in childbirth in antiquity was substantial. As Tikva Frymer-Kensky suggests, 'It may be that, like the person who has touched death, the person who has experienced birth has been at the boundaries of life/non-life and therefore cannot directly re-enter the community. She therefore must undergo a long period of transition before she can reapproach the sacred' (Frymer-Kensky 1983: 401). The parturient is integral to the death–life cycle, the cycle of mortality which distinguishes man from God and remains a constant source of impurity (Wright 1992: 738–41; Maccoby 1999: 49–50). The new mother, more, than anyone else, actively participates in this process.

The Qumran tendency to cloud the distinction between ritual and moral purity is apparent in the matter of sexual discharges. Although Leviticus prescribes a concluding sacrifice for the *zab* and *zabah* at the end of their purification, the disease is usually considered a ritual rather than a moral impurity (Lev. 15.14-15). The Damascus Document associates the disease with 'lascivious thoughts' and lists the *zab* in a catalogue of sinners (4Q270 9 ii) (Baumgarten 1994b: 273–75; 1999b: 87–88, 93). His condition is, according to the author, due to improper sexual stimuli (4Q266, 4Q272). As with the leper, the *zab*'s questionable state of health was considered by the Scroll author to be a divine retribution for sin. Indeed, biblical precedent for the connection between flux and sin is found in David's curse upon Joab: due to his murderous vengeance there would always be a *zab* among the general's descendants (2 Sam. 3.29). This contrasts with the explanations of Rabbinic sages, which limit the definition of flux to a great degree and state that if the condition resulted from sexual fantasies it was not considered the biblical disease (m. *Zab.* 2.2).[5]

The removal of persons with sexual flows from any active role within society underscores the perception that bodily discharges are dangerous and ritually contagious to the community. This negative stance toward discharges exists in many cultures. In tribal societies, where a woman was often pregnant, menstruation was a sign of death, the loss of the expected child. The woman who was menstruating was not producing life, but rather losing life forces.

On a practical note, sexual flows also repel, probably because they are simply messy. They ooze over a period of time and are easily deposited on beds, chairs and other seats, soiling both them and those that use them. As noted above, the line between ritual and physical impurity is sometimes blurred. Excrement, because of its very nature as waste, is often considered a matter of ritual impurity as well as physical cleanliness.

5. This alleviation may be due to the hopelessness of remedying the situation, especially with the lack of the Temple for the concluding sacrifice of the *zab*'s purification week (Lev. 15.14). For further discussion, cf. Harrington 1993: 259–60.

Further Reading

Baumgarten, J.M.

1994b '*Zab* Impurity in Qumran and Rabbinic Law', *JJS* 45: 273–78.

1995a 'A Fragment on Fetal Life and Pregnancy in 4Q270', in *Pomegranates and Golden Bells*, ed. D. Wright (Winona Lake, IN: Eisenbrauns): 445–48.

1999b *Qumran Cave 4 XXV: Halakhic Texts, Discoveries in the Judaean Desert XXXV* (Oxford: Clarendon Press).

Cook, L.A.

1999 'Body Language: Women's Rituals of Purification in the Bible and Mishnah', in *Women and Water: Menstruation in Jewish Life and Law*, ed. Rahel Wasserfall (Waltham, MA: Brandeis University Press): 40–59.

Elgvin, T.

1999 '472a. 4QHalakha C', in *Qumran Cave 4 XXV: Halakhic Texts, Discoveries in the Judaean Desert XXXV* (Oxford: Clarendon Press): 155–56.

Greenberg, M.

1995 'The Etymology of *Niddah* (Heb.) "(Menstrual) Impurity"', in *Solving Riddles and Untying Knots* (Winona Lake, IN: Eisenbrauns): 69–77.

Meacham, T.

1999 'An Abbreviated History of the Development of the Jewish Menstrual Laws', in *Women and Water: Menstruation in Jewish Life and Law*, ed. R. Wasserfall (Waltham, MA: Brandeis University Press): 23–39.

Milgrom, J.

1991 *Leviticus 1–16*, The Anchor Bible 3A (Garden City, NY: Doubleday).

Schiffman, L.H.

1992 'Laws Pertaining to Women in the Temple Scroll', in *The Dead Sea Scrolls: Forty Years of Research*, eds. D. Dimant and U. Rappaport (Leiden: E.J. Brill): 210–28.

6

OUTSIDERS

1. Introduction

The distinction between insider and outsider to the group at Qumran was expressed in terms of purity. Labelling outsiders ritually as well as morally impure helped to preserve the group's identity as a community set apart to maintain holiness in Israel. The idea that outsiders were morally impure, while members of the sect were holy, was reinforced physically by the label of ritual impurity.

2. Historical Antecedents

2.1. Bible

Although the moral impurity of non-Israelites is denounced throughout the Hebrew Bible, one would be hard-pressed to make a case for their ritual defilement and contagion. Gentiles are not a category of impurity anywhere in the Torah. According to the Pentateuch, not all outsiders are forbidden into the community; only marriages with the seven Canaanite nations are strictly prohibited (Deut. 7.1-4; also cf. 23.3, 8). And, nowhere is this said to be on account of ritual impurity; rather, it is on account of idolatrous influence (Deut. 7.4). In fact, war captives can be taken as wives, and non-Israelites may live among Israel as resident aliens. If they were inherently impure, Gentiles could not be adopted by the Israelite community.[1] The

1. Hayes 2002: 21 points to the integration of the *ger* (a non-Israelite resident) in Israelite society as proof that he could not be intrinsically impure: Rahabites dwell among Israel (Josh. 6.25) and are brought to the Temple (Jer. 35); Gibeonites draw water and bring wood for the community and 'for the altar of the Lord'; *netinim* are foreign temple servants; both Israel and the *ger* can bring a *ḥatta't* for unintentional

universal ban against Gentile marriages is introduced by Ezra and even then it is not due to ritual impurity (Hayes 1999: 3–36).

Nevertheless, although the concern is to vilify idolatry and immorality, biblical language often employs the metaphor of impurity in its descriptions of these sins. The Torah describes the following sins as defiling: sexual sins (Lev. 18.24-30); idolatry (Lev. 19.31; 20.1-3) and murder (Num. 35.33-34). The prophets continue the association of immorality and impurity. Jeremiah regards Israel's impurity stains as too deep to be washed away (Jer. 2.22); sinners remind Ezekiel of a menstruous woman (Ezek. 36.17); Zechariah promises an atoning fountain of purification in the messianic era (Zech. 13.1). These metaphors of impurity are easily concretized in the minds of later readers, and hence passages like these were a seedbed for the later notion of the ritual impurity of Gentiles.

2.2. Second Temple Judaism

In the Second Temple period more restrictions with regard to Gentiles begin to appear in the texts and the language of impurity is employed. Marriages with Gentiles are forbidden by several texts. Some writers reveal a decided bias against the whole concept of conversion. According to *Jubilees*, for example, there is no way properly to contract marriage with a Gentile, even when there has been sexual intercourse and even if the Gentile is willing to be circumcised and join Israel. Nevertheless, Gentiles may live in the community as *gerim* (resident aliens; Hayes 2002: 77, 81). Several texts reveal a certain distrust and antipathy toward non-Jews. In the latter category are works like Psalms of Solomon and *Jubilees* which depict Gentiles negatively due to idolatry and the oppression of foreign conquerors (cf. Pss. of Sol. 2.1-20; *Jub.* 23.23; see 'Rationale' below).

'Impure' becomes a label for Gentiles stemming originally from their idolatry. The Torah labels idolatry, and, in particular, Molech worship, 'impure', but *Jubilees* extends this impurity from the practice of idolatry to the idolater, i.e. the Gentile (Milgrom 1993: 283). Jews begin to avoid not only contact with the sin but with the sinner. Physical consequences now apply for mere contact with Gentiles, not just for participation in their idolatry. People, not just principles and behaviour, are considered impure. The impurity becomes located not only in Gentile practices but also in

sin (Num. 15.25ff); Ittai the Gittite is allowed to fight in holy war (2 Sam. 15); commerce, even to selling foodstuffs, existed between Israelites and Gentiles (Neh. 10.32; 13.16) and peoples of the land (Neh. 10.32); the stranger even gets an allotment of the land (Ezek. 47.21-23).

Gentile bodies, contact with which results in physical restrictions and negative consequences. Eating with Gentiles causes those who eat with them to share in their impurity (*Jub.* 22.17).[2] *Jubilees* even attributes defilement to a father who has allowed his daughter to marry a Gentile (*Jub.* 30.10). The Second Temple complex included the Court of the Gentiles which barred them from the sanctuary proper. While it can be argued that this exclusion was because of Gentiles' low status, impurity was a concern too. Josephus, for example, refers to the exclusion of foreigners from the Temple as a 'law of purification' (*War* 5.194).

3. Attitude towards Gentiles at Qumran

Restrictions on social interaction with Gentiles abound in the Qumran texts. A Jew may not send a Gentile to do his business on the Sabbath (CD 11.2). It is considered improper to spend the Sabbath in a place near pagans (CD 11.14). A Jew should not sell clean animals, servants or agriculture to Gentiles (CD 12.8-11).[3] Metals used in pagan cults are labelled impure and may not be reused (4Q268 1 ii 8-10; cf. Rabbinic allowance to 'nullify' idolatrous metals, m. *AZ* 3.2; Baumgarten 1996: 131). Sacrifices brought by Gentiles are especially repulsive: 'And concerning the sacrifice of the Gentiles: we are of the opinion that they sacrifice to the ... that is like [a woman] who whored with him' (MMT B 8–9). This is opposite the Rabbinic position, which does accept sacrifices from Gentiles, although the subject was controversial in the Second Temple period (m. *Zeb.* 4.5; *War* 2.409-10; cf. Num. 16.15-16).

The attitude of the Qumran sect toward the *ger*, the person of Gentile ancestry who wishes to live among Israel, reveals the extent of its antipathy towards and mistrust of Gentiles. The Temple Scroll restricts the *ger* from entering into the middle court of the Temple until the fourth generation (11Q19 39.5-7). 4QFlorilegium seems to reject any kind of conversion: the Ammonite, Moabite, bastard, alien and *ger* will never enter the messianic sanctuary 'for my holy ones are there' (4Q174 1.3-4). Since the

2. Whether or not the author regards this impurity as moral as well as ritual has been debated, cf. Hayes 2002: 25; Werman 1997: 16, 21. While Gentile ritual impurity may not be the basis for the laws, it is still a concern.

3. Even with the above restrictions, Jews are admonished by the Scrolls not to treat Gentiles unfairly so as not to give them a reason to blaspheme the God of Israel (CD 12.6-8). Gentile servants in Jewish homes may not be sold to pagans (CD 12.10-11).

community at Qumran identified itself as a living sanctuary (1QS 4.6; 1Q34 3 ii 6 *bis*; 4Q174 1.6), in anticipation of the messianic temple, the implication is that the *ger* is not welcomed. As L. Schiffman says: 'The sectarians saw the proselytes as constituting a class within their society of a status different than that of full Israelites. In this respect, they agreed with an approach known to have been held by a minority of *tanna'im* (t. *Qid.* 5.1)' (Schiffman 1997: 169–70; cf. Lieberman 1952: 200 n 8).

The Qumran group was apparently celibate, but marriage of Jews to Gentiles, even those willing to convert, is not welcomed in the larger sectarian community (Schiffman 1997: 162; Hayes 2002: 82–90). According to Deuteronomy, certain classes of people may not 'enter the congregation of the LORD' (Deut. 23.2-4). According to MMT, this law forbids Jews to intermarry with any non-Jews, '. . . one must not let them be united (with an Israelite) and make them [one bone . . .' (MMT B 44; cf. 4Q174 1.3-4; 11Q19 2.12-15; 57.15-17).[4] MMT B 75–78 uses the metaphor of mixing animal species, forbidden by the Torah, to denounce marriage with Gentiles (cf. also lines 80–82). Conversion according to the Temple Scroll is a difficult process and the rules governing it seem aimed at precluding the notion altogether (see below; cf. 11Q19 63.15, see below; Schiffman 1992: 210–28).

The exclusion of proselytes as desirable marriage partners may be due to the sect's priestly orientation. D. Schwartz explains: 'Those for whom descent constitutes their own special status in Israel will tend to apply that same criterion to Israel as well, thus excluding proselytes' (Schwartz 1990: 165). According to the sect, all members are *ʿadat 'anshe tamim ha-qodesh*, 'the congregation of the men of perfect holiness' (CD 20.2-7; 1QS 9.20; See Chapter 1). As if it were the Temple, the community adopts priestly standards with regard to marriage as well as several other matters (e.g. excluding physically impaired persons and adopting stringent purity rules; CD 15.15-16).

Nevertheless, the sect does include *gerim* as a sub-group within the community, for indeed the *ger* is a biblical institution. The Qumran texts allow the *ger* some degree of participation in the community (CD 14.4-6 allows participation in meetings; 11Q19 40.6 allows *gerim* into the sanctuary courtyard after the third or fourth generation; cf. also 4Q169 3-4 ii 9). However, because of their Gentile ancestry, they comprise a separate group which is not fully assimilated into the community of Israel.

4. According to C. Hayes and M. Himmelfarb, intermarriage between Jew and Gentile *per se* was not a serious problem in the period leading up to the Maccabean Revolt; rather the problem for the sectarians was marriage between Gentile proselytes and Jews (Hayes 2002: 83).

The Qumranite *ger* is more like the biblical resident alien than the full-fledged convert to Judaism.[5]

4. Outsider Impurity at Qumran

While there is no question that Gentiles were looked down upon by the Qumran community, do they by physical contact cause the sectarians to become ritually impure? From the texts of the Qumran Community it appears that outsiders, both Jew and Gentile, were considered morally and  ritually impure. That is, not only were outsiders considered sinners in need of atonement but their state of defilement could contaminate persons, food and certain other items, resulting in an impurity that had to be physically washed away. The sections below divide the laws of impurity of outsiders into two categories: (1) general impurity laws regarding outsiders, and (2) laws specifically related to Gentile impurity.

4.1. General impurity laws regarding outsiders

Purity restrictions on food reveal that non-sectarians were thought to contaminate pure food and persons belonging to the sect. Qumran authors restrict outsiders from eating or handling the pure food and property of the sect (1QS 6.20; 7.20; 4Q284a 1.2-4). As discussed earlier, the food of the sect must be eaten in a state of purity, and is even referred to as *ha-tohorah*, 'the purity' (1QS 5.13; 8.17; CD 9.21). Any contact between impurity and pure food would defile it (4Q514; 4Q512 col. xi, frag. 9). A good parallel for the sectarian attitude toward food and outsiders is found in the Mishnah; the *Ḥaberim* (a group of Pharisees) do not want the *ʿAm ha'areṣ* (Jewish commoners untrustworthy in matters of purity and tithes) to defile pure food. They do not allow the *ʿAm ha'areṣ* to eat or even touch pure food (Alon 1977; 205–23; Harrington 1995: 42–54).

The process of initiating outsiders into the sect reveals the physical consequence of their impurity. Newcomers to the sect may not eat of the communal food until they are completely purified. Candidates are examined for purity (1QS 6.16-22) and after one year's probation they are allowed to eat the communal, pure food; after two years they may drink the community's drink (1QS 6.20; 7.20; cf. *War* 2.123, 138; CD 15.14-15).

5. According to J. Milgrom (1982: 169–76), the term *ger* in the post-biblical period usually refers 'not merely to a sojourner who observes prohibitive commandments [a usage retained by Judith; see 4: 10-11 and chapter 5] but to a religious convert who takes on all of the obligations, responsibilities and privileges of a member of the Israelite community'.

This process reveals stages in the removal of 'outsider impurity'. Those outside the sect were ritually impure 'while the new member gradually became less and less impure through the initiation process ...' (García Martínez and Trebolle-Barrera 1995: 153).

It stands to reason that most people attracted to the stringent Qumran version of Judaism would be Jews. And there can be no doubt that these candidates membership would have been considered ritually impure by the sect. Since Israel is under a biblical mandate to purify itself from impurity and since the sect regarded only its interpretation of purity as valid, Jews who were not members were considered still impure. The Community Rule is adamant that no amount of purification can be effective if one has not been obedient to God's will, of course as interpreted by the sect (cf. 1QS 3.3-6). Thus, purification rites conducted outside the bounds of the community were considered invalid (Taylor 1997: 77). Josephus states that Essenes even 'sacrifice separately', which probably means that they worshipped in a separate area at the Temple (Baumgarten 1977: 62). Such designations as *tohorat ṣedek* (4Q512 40-41) and *tohorat 'emet* (4Q284 3.4) reinforce the sectarians' attitude that only purity according to their particular definition was valid.

The concern that outsiders would contaminate pure food began from the time of harvest. Not only outsiders but even those candidates to the sect who were not yet full members were forbidden to harvest produce lest their impurity be transferred to the crop:

> [If] their [ju]ice comes out wh[en he pre]sses them all, and they be gathered by [one] who has not been brou[ght into the co]venant. And if they press [olives in the olive pr]ess, let him b[y] no [mean]s defile them by opening them before he pours [them into the press. Let them be squee]zed in purity, and when their processing is [finish]ed they will be ea[ten in purity]. (4Q284a 1.2-8; tr. Baumgarten 1999b: 132)

The possessions of outsiders too are impure; restrictions are not limited to food. The author of the Community Rule warns the sect about the outsider's moral and ritual impurity:

> No one should associate with him in his work or in his possessions in order not to encumber him with blameworthy sin; rather he should remain at a distance from him in every task ... All his deeds are impurity before him and there is impurity in all his possessions ... (1QS 5.14-20)

There is a concern here for contagion, i.e. that one will contract the impurity of the outsider even by touching his possessions. It appears that the label of ritual impurity is being applied here as a tool to prevent social contact with outsiders altogether.

The impurity of sinners had to be removed by both atonement and ablutions before they were allowed to eat pure food at the communal table. According to the Community Rule, an enrollee was not permitted to eat of the community's pure food, lest he ritually defile it: 'He must not enter the water in order to touch the "purity" [= pure food] of the men of holiness. For they cannot be purified unless they turn away from their wickedness, for [he remains] impure among all those who transgress His words' (1QS 5.13-14). The outsider is considered impure and in need of purification, by both atonement and ablutions, before he may enter the community (Klawans 2000: 86; Newton 1985: 47–49; Baumgarten 1999a: 211; 1992b: 201).

According to Josephus, even after entry into the community ritual purity was used by the Essenes to mark moral development. He explains that internal barriers between senior and junior levels of Essenes were enforced with ritual purity concerns. That is, a member of lower standing, e.g. a candidate to the group, would make a member of higher standing impure simply by touching him (*War* 2.150). This text is interesting because it shows that a physical consequence applies to those who carry low moral rankings.

4.2. Gentile Outsiders

Scholars have noted that in the matter of impurity of outsiders, one should distinguish between Jewish and Gentile outsiders (Hayes 2002: 65–66). Gentiles are not a source of impurity in the Torah, nor are they avoided in First Temple times because of ritual contamination. The Rabbis note this distinction when they say that Gentiles are not liable for keeping the Jewish impurity system (t. *Zab.* 2.1), even though they did ascribe a separate category of impurity to Gentiles. Thus, some scholars would apply outsider impurity to Jewish outsiders and novitiates only. Nevertheless, there are several factors which support the notion of Gentile impurity among the Qumran sectarians.

A brief look at the external evidence for Gentile impurity in early Judaism outside of Qumran is important before turning to the data of the Scrolls. Several Rabbinic texts regard Gentiles as outside of the Jewish purity system but still impure simply because they are Gentiles.[6] The

6. The notion that outsiders generate ritual impurity is not unique to the Second Temple period. Jacob Milgrom cites Sefer Eldad ha-Dani, of Ethiopian Jews, which reads, 'one who touches a person of another religion or any defiling object (or person) may not eat anything until evening and must be quarantined for the entire day. In the evening he immerses himself in water and becomes pure.' Another sect, the Melchisedecitae, a Christian sect in Phrygia, avoided outsiders and refused to take anything from them (Baumgarten 1977: 97).

Mishnah requires ritual purification of all proselytes, stating, 'He that separates himself from the foreskin is as one who separates himself from a grave' (m. *Pes.* 8.8). The Eighteen Decrees regard them impure like a *zab*: 'Gentiles and a resident alien do not defile by reason of a flux, but although they do not defile because of a flux, they are impure in all respects like those who suffer a flux, and *terumah* [the agricultural contribution to the priests] is burned on their account' (t. *Zab.* 2.1; *Sif. mes. zab. par.* 1.1; b. *Shab.* 17b; b. *AZ* 46b; y. *Shab.* 1.3).[7]

Nevertheless, the Rabbis are not consistent on the degree of the Gentiles' impurity, and the matter is treated as a Rabbinic enactment, not a biblical decree. As G. Alon says, it is a concept 'which existed in the nation from early times, even though not all agreed to it, nor did the practice at all times conform to it, nor did the Sages rule according to it' (Alon 1977: 147–48; cf. also b. *Shab.* 17b; Halevi 1967: 1.591–93; Weiss 1904: 129; but see criticism by Hayes 2002: 36, who dates the notion to the first century). It is also the case that not all Rabbis viewed Gentiles as contaminating. The Talmud states in one place that even holy food is not made unacceptable by contact with a Gentile (b. *Nid.* 34a). Significantly, Gentile impurity is in the category of Rabbinic enactments, which are theoretically reversible (Hayes 2002: 36).

The presence of a notion of Gentile impurity in primary Rabbinic texts lends credibility to the statements both within and outside of the Qumran corpus that the sect regarded Gentiles as ritually impure. The Mishnah outlines a view of purity that, while it has been regarded as strict by many, comes nowhere near the stringency revealed at Qumran. If the early Rabbis thought it necessary to enact a decree of Gentile impurity, certainly the notion fits with the much stricter stance toward purity found among the Qumran sectarians, a group which in fact separated completely from the general population in Palestine (Licht 1965b: 44–62).

The clearest statement on Gentile impurity with regard to the sect comes from Josephus. He writes explicitly that after contact with foreigners (not just Jewish outsiders), Essenes bathed (*War* 2.150). Some scholars have tried to dismiss this statement on the basis that Josephus is not always credible. However, this is just the kind of statement that should be taken seriously. As is well known, Josephus sometimes slants his

7. Nevertheless, because of Num. 31.19, in which Gentiles (Midianites) contaminated Israelites, the Rabbis concede that Gentile corpses are contaminating but only to Jews, Maccoby 1999: 11; also cf. Num. 19.14, which is inclusive of all dead human beings, '*met le-kol nefesh 'adam*', instead of specifically Israelites.

presentation of Judaism to gain favour with his Gentile readers. A statement that Gentiles were considered defiling by contact does nothing to help his presentation of the Jews. In addition, Luke states that 'the Jews' washed themselves after contact with Gentiles to rid themselves of ritual impurity (Acts 10.38). Even if this text is an exaggeration, and does not mean that all Jews considered Gentiles impure, the fact that the author says 'the Jews' indicates a widespread concern regarding Gentile impurity and makes the statement of Josephus regarding the Essenes appear completely reasonable.

Now let us look at internal evidence. The question is, do the Qumran texts support the claims of these non-sectarian authors? Do these statements make sense in light of the Qumran texts? It is important to recognize at the outset that nowhere do the sectarian authors distinguish between the impurity of Jewish outsiders as opposed to Gentile ones. People who live outside the sect's boundaries are impure. In fact, as 1QH puts it, anyone 'born of woman ... a structure of dust shaped with water, his base is the guilt of sin, vile unseemliness, source of impurity ...' (1QH 13.21). Here humans are identified with impurity, which is inherent in their structure (García Martínez 1995: 155). Indeed, according to the Community Rule, whoever does not join the sect is hopelessly 'defiled, defiled shall he be' (1QS 3.4-5). This text sets forth the difference between the purity of those who have pledged themselves to holiness and the impurity of those who trespass the words of God and have not joined the community (1QS 5.13-14; cf. 1Q28a 2.3-5; 1QH 6.20f; Hubner 1992: 741–45). A fundamental reason for the existence of the community, according to the Damascus Document, is to 'separate unclean from clean and differentiate between holy and common' (CD 6.15-18).

The authors of many Qumran texts regarded themselves as the true Israel, Sons of Light, engaged in a bipolar struggle against the Sons of Darkness (1QM 1.1, 5; 1QS; 1QH; 4Q266 1 i 1). False Israelites, those who would not obey the 'glorious voice' and accept the 'profound things' taught by the angels, are sinners in darkness along with Gentiles (1QM 10.11). The Admonition section of the Damascus Document explains that the divine covenant with Israel has been transferred to the righteous remnant, i.e. the members of the Qumran sect. The true Israel then is comprised only of those who join the sect (Schiffman 2000a: 389). Thus, for the most part, non-sectarian Jews and Gentiles are in the same category. Rules are established to maintain barriers between sectarian and non-sectarian more than between Jew and non-Jew. The fact that these rules restrict not only immoral behaviour but also contact with food and property suggests a concern for ritual impurity as well.

A Gentile who converted to Judaism and wished to join the sect would certainly have to perform all the initiatory purifications described above in the entry process. Indeed the biblical *ger* was required to maintain the purity laws of Israel (Lev. 17.15-16: Num. 15.16; Milgrom 2000: 1496–97).

It can be argued that since Gentiles clearly carry a moral deficiency, according to the Qumran sect, they must also be ritually impure. For the sect, atonement and ritual purity went hand in hand. Several authors present the problem of impurity not as two types of impurity so much as one problem requiring both spiritual and physical purification (Baumgarten 1999a: 211–12; Schiffman 1983b: 216; Klawans 2000: 82). The Community Rule states that 'impurity is inherent in all transgressors of divine law' (1QS 5.4), and the author requires both water ablutions and repentance for atonement (1QS 5.13-14). The author of 4Q512 does not acknowledge atonement until after immersion (4Q512 10-11 x 2-5; 29-32 vii 5 and 16 viii; Baumgarten 1999a: 205–206). Purifying persons were apparently not considered fit to offer a blessing to God until after ritual purification, for it is after they immerse, while still standing in the water, that they offer the blessing (4Q512 11 x; cf. also Rabbinic practice b. *Ber.* 51a; b. *Pes.* 7b; t. *Yad.* 2.20).[8] Additionally, as noted above, ritual purity and access to pure food were denied to the disobedient (1QS 7.2-21; 8.22-24; *War* 2.143). The distinction between sin and impurity is blurred. (This admixture of ritual and moral defilement is also present in some non-Qumranic texts of this era, cf. Sib. Or. 4.165; T. Levi 2.3.)

Let us look now at Qumran texts that refer to the impurity of Gentiles. Both marriage with Gentiles as well as simple contact between Gentiles and pure food and/or persons are labelled impure. Marriage with Gentile women is referred to in MMT as *to'ebah*, 'an abomination', as well as *tum'ah*, 'impurity'. The author says his group has physically separated from the majority of the nation because, at least in part, the latter have married impure Gentile women (MMT C 49). In fact, MMT explicitly connects intermarriage with impurity, stating that it 'pollutes holy seed' (B 81). As in the Temple Scroll, examined below, the impurity here need not be understood simply as symbolic; indeed, it has caused a physical separation (cf. Klawans 2000: 133).

8. E. Eshel (1997: 5) notes the difficulty of ascertaining what prayers precede or follow immersion. However, it is clear that the act of atonement is not completed until the immersion has taken place. While pleas for forgiveness may precede the immersion, thanksgiving for atonement granted comes only after the immersion.

The Temple Scroll applies impurity language to Gentile wives in an effort to erect a physical barrier to intermarriage. This is evident in the author's rewrite of the biblical restrictions on female war captives. Deuteronomy states, 'you shall bring her into your house, and she shall trim her hair, pare her nails, and discard her captive's garb. She shall spend a month's time in your house lamenting her father and mother; after that you may come to her and possess her, and she shall be your wife' (Deut. 21.10-14). After the phrase, 'she shall be your wife', the Temple Scroll adds, 'But she may not touch pure food, *tohorah,* for seven years. Nor shall she eat a *shelamim* offering until seven years pass, then she shall eat' (col. 63.15). Once again, the matter of pure food becomes a delineation of outsider and insider. In order to preserve the holy community and prevent intermarriage with Gentiles, the author uses the tool and label of ritual impurity.

In addition to the general restrictions on outsiders with regard to pure food (discussed above), the Qumran authors explicitly target Gentile women who have married priests. These wives may not eat or even touch priestly food. According to 4Q513, when daughters of priests marry non-Jews their whole families (including the priest) are denied eating priestly contributions or even touching them. The mixture of ordinary food with priestly food results in *ʿavon zimmah,* the 'sin of immorality' (4Q513 11.3). According to 4Q251 frag. 16, a priest's household (including wives, daughters and even slaves) may usually eat of his food gifts. However, a priest's wife who was an immoral woman or the daughter of a forbidden union may not eat of her husband's food gifts or even touch them (4Q251 16.2-3; Baumgarten 1999b: 44). Thus, if a priest married a Gentile woman, she could not prepare or eat his food.

Some might attribute this exclusion to the fear that the forbidden woman will not serve food within the rules of *kashrut;* that is, the outsider will not prepare food in accordance with Jewish law. This may be a legitimate concern but it is not expressed. Immorality seems to be the factor which generates the restriction and the ritual impurity.

Finally, one text refers explicitly to the impurity of Gentile persons (Baumgarten 1992a: 512–13). According to 4Q266 5 ii, 5-7: '[Anyone of the] sons of Aaron who was in captivity among the Gentiles [ ] *lhḻllh btm'tm,* "to profane him with their impurity" may not approach the [holy] service [ ] within the curtain *vacat* and may not eat the [most] holy offerings ...' (cf. also 4Q267 6 ii 5-9; CD 14.15; *Jub.* 1.13; Baumgarten 1996: 9–11). Thus, a priest who had been in Gentile captivity was assumed to have become defiled by contact with Gentiles and, in consequence, was disqualified for Temple service.[9]

In sum, according to the Qumran sect all outsiders carry both a moral and ritual impurity. First, the group divided the world into sons of light (the sect) and sons of darkness (outsiders); outsiders (both Jew and Gentile) are restricted in terms of impure persons, food and property. Secondly, there is a general conflation of moral and ritual impurity in the sect's ideology; where there is moral impurity, ritual impurity is applied as well. Third, marriages with Gentile proselytes are constrained by the impurity restrictions on them, expressed in terms of food and drink. Fourth, the impurity of Gentiles is the stated reason for disallowing priests who have been detained in foreign lands. Finally, extra-biblical texts confirm the existence of the notion of Gentile impurity (both ritual and moral) in the Second Temple period, and in particular among the Essenes.

5. Rationale

It is apparent from the above examples that labelling the outsider impure at Qumran is an effective tool in reinforcing the barriers between members and non-members of the sect. Scholars tell us that impurity labels enforce social boundaries (Wright 1992: 739–41). If one is not allowed to eat with or even touch another person, social intercourse between the two is automatically diminished. Preserving group identity then becomes the overall reason for labelling outsiders impure.

Anthropologists have shown that when a group is a hard-pressed minority, it becomes more careful to maintain its boundaries, both those of the community as well as those of the body, which becomes a symbol of the community. That which enters the body becomes a symbol of those who enter the community, and that which leaves the body is symbolic of those expelled from the community, and so it is a polluting agent (Douglas 1966: 124; 1975: 269). Thus, restriction and expulsion are expressed in terms of ritual impurity: food and drink owned or handled by outsiders become identified with the outsiders themselves. Just as they must be expelled, so items which represent them or come under their control must be eliminated (Regev 2000a: 238).

9. See Hayes 2002: 202–203, who examines Rabbinic sources and concludes that indiscriminate burial in Gentile areas is what makes them impure and contaminates Jews entering them (cf. 11Q19 48.11-12). However, as J. Baumgarten notes, according to the Mishnah, the principle of overhang does not apply in Gentile areas; thus walking over a grave would not contaminate a person (private communication).

Let us examine the rationale for both categories of impure outsiders: Jews and Gentiles. Jewish outsiders are impure because they do not conform to the Torah's purity system as interpreted by the sectarians. Gentiles, it could be argued, are not susceptible to the Jewish purity code. However, there is no doubt that Jews were responsible for the Torah's laws of ritual purity. Non-sectarian Jews were by definition impure since they did not purify themselves according to the interpretations presented by the Qumran authors.

The impurity of Gentile outsiders is more complicated. As we have discussed above, the Qumran sectarians considered Gentile outsiders impure and even Gentile proselytes appear to carry at least a temporary, residual impurity. There are at least two reasons. First of all, Gentiles represented foreign rule and oppression and so represent a physical threat. *Pesher Habakkuk* graphically portrays the barbarian character of the 'Kittim', apparently a code name for the Romans (1QpHab 3.4-14). The War Scroll promises complete eradication of the wickedness of the enemies of God (1QM 10.10-11). E. Regev, after examining the passages requiring purification after contact with Gentiles in Second Temple sources as well as Rabbinic sources concludes that 'this halakhic concept emerged before the Maccabean revolt, but spread due to the struggle against the Seleucids and the Hellenistic population in the Land of Israel' (Regev 2000a: 221). Indeed, the Hellenistic period was characterized for the Jews by oppression. Some rulers even demanded worship. Antiochus IV, of the second century BCE, outlawed circumcision and forbade obedience to the laws of Judaism; war ensued. Romans followed the Greeks with an iron fist.

Hayes sheds light on this discussion from her study of Rabbinic texts. As noted, Rabbinic texts are inconsistent on the matter of Gentile impurity, some Rabbis regarding them as impure at different levels of impurity, and others claiming that Gentiles are not susceptible to impurity. Hayes concludes that the label of impurity tends to be applied in situations involving violent or threatening Gentiles. 'As a general rule, the laws of ritual impurity are applied in cases that envisage an interaction with an untrustworthy or hostile Gentile ... their primary application appears to have been the delineation of (perhaps, a reminder of the need for) a barrier between Jews and Gentiles whose intentions were hostile or threatening in some way' (Hayes 2002: 143).

A second reason for the impurity of Gentile outsiders is the biblical emphasis on the impurity of idolatry, extended by the sectarians to the impurity of idolaters. As noted above, many sins are referred to as impure by the biblical author. Idolatry is a threat to holiness and, by extension so are those who worship idols. The literature of Qumran reveals a low estimate of Gentile culture. The Temple Scroll disparages Gentiles because they bury the dead in their homes (11Q19 48.12), they subscribe to the cult of Molech which requires child sacrifice, and they engage in various acts of necromancy (11Q19 60.17-19). It is a small step from labelling idolatry impure to labelling the idolater impure. The biblical text gives birth to concepts which sprout into full plants by later authors, who literalize the Torah's comments regarding moral impurity and shape it into a full-blown concept of Gentile ritual impurity.

By interacting with Gentiles, one might be influenced to compromise the worship of Yahweh with pagan practices and even participate in wholesale idolatry. For both biblical and post-biblical Jewish texts, a primary concern seems to be that social interaction will lead to intermarriage (Milgrom 1993: 282). The Torah warns:

> You must not make a covenant with the inhabitants of the land, for they will lust after their gods and sacrifice to their gods and invite you, and you will eat of their sacrifices. And when you take wives from among their daughters for your sons, their daughters will lust after their gods and will cause your sons to lust after their gods. (Exod. 34.15-16; cf. Isa. 52.1; Joel 4.17)

Eating together leads to intermarriage which leads to idolatry. Maimonides' explanation for the Rabbinic enactment of Gentile impurity can be helpful for describing the attitude of the Qumran authors: impurity labels are a 'fence' which guards against assimilation by restricting contact with Gentiles (Maimonides, *Code, Tum'at Met* 1.14; *Sif. meṣ. zab.* 1.1; b. *Nid.* 34a cf. also Letter of Aristeas 142). As noted above, the Qumranites protest against taking Gentiles, even proselytes, as wives, and they express their concern in terms of impurity.

At the very least, interacting with Gentiles puts a Jew in danger of unwittingly contributing to idolatry. For example, by selling animals to Gentiles, one might be providing pagan sacrifices. This seems to be the concern of CD 12.8-9: in order to avoid contributing to impurity, clean birds/beasts could not be sold to Gentiles, nor could sacrifices be accepted from them (cf. also MMT B 8–9).[10] This was the reasoning of the early Sages as well: with the exception of small cattle, it was forbidden to sell to the Gentiles items which they would use for idolatry (m. *AZ* 1.5-6). Foreign oil too was banned by the Rabbis, probably because of its association with idolatry (Baumgarten 1977: 97).

Finally, outsider impurity reinforces the notion that insiders are

10. The early Sages too probably refused to sell clean fowl to Gentiles for fear that they might sacrifice them to idols (cf. m. *AZ* 1.5, Schiffman, 'Legislation', 385). The Mishnah is more lenient with regard to selling cattle and sheep to Gentiles (cf. m. *AZ* 1.6; m. *Pes.* 4.3).

connected with the God of holiness and life. The Bible associates false gods with death and oblivion, whereas Yahweh is a living God, in fact, the creator of life, and only the living can properly praise him (Ps. 36.9; Isa. 45.5-21; Jer. 10.10; cf. Gen. 2.7).[11] J. Milgrom has already noted many correlations between particular impurities and death (Milgrom 1991: 766–68, 1000–1002). Those who have not accepted the true path to holiness, guided by the purity laws and other precepts of the sect, are still in the realm of impurity and death (see Chapter 1 for more on the link between death and impurity at Qumran). Keeping the purity laws of the Torah reminded the Qumranites that they were separated from those in sin and darkness and committed to the maintenance of purity which embraces the God of holiness and life.

Like other impurity bearers, the outsider too is associated with the dead. Non-sectarian Jews are simply not in compliance with laws of God and so are considered to be not only in a perpetual state of impurity but also on the road to 'death' (Deut. 30.15-20). Gentiles represent the foreign, dead

gods they worship as opposed to Judaism's one, living God, thus they too are in the realm of death, and at Qumran this was marked with the label of ritual impurity. Scholars have emphasized that in Israelite cosmology it was considered vitally important to maintain the structure of the universe by keeping all distinctions (boundaries) firm; no individual who has had contact with the world of death can be part of life. As T. Frymer-Kensky says, he must therefore stay in limbo until purification will 'enable him to rejoin the life-group' (Frymer-Kensky 1983: 399–414; cf. Douglas 1966: 53).

An added Qumran distinction on the impurity of outsiders is that the sect appears to require all novitiates to purify themselves with *me niddah*, the special purification water used for those defiled by contact with a dead body (Baumgarten 1999b: 84). The Community Rule describes the purification of the penitent like so: 'It is by humbling his soul to all God's statutes that his flesh can be cleansed by sprinkling with waters of purification [*me niddah*] and by sanctifying himself with waters of purity' (1QS 3.7-9). The symbolism is striking; the candidate to the sect is crossing from death and impurity to life and purity by joining the group.[12] As an outsider he was living as a corpse in the realm of the dead,

11. The Rabbis champion this notion repeatedly, cf. b. *BB* 10a; b. *Ber.* 33a; b. *Meg.* 14a; *Lev. R.* 6.6; 19.2. For fuller discussion of the connection between purity/life and impurity/death, see J. Milgrom 1991: 766–68, 1000–1002.

12. Ringgren 1986: 288 notes that in Egypt the hieroglyphs 'life' and 'happiness' flow from the purification flasks which purify the king. So also the purification of the dead brings ritual purity and new life.

but the sect has given him the opportunity to live again. The later Rabbis, too, obliged proselytes to immerse in water as part of their conversion rites as they took on a new life within Israel.

Ritual purification with *me niddah* as an initiation rite is attested in Judaism as far back as the biblical period. Levites were inducted into service with purification rites: 'The LORD said to Moses: Take the Levites from among the other Israelites and make them ritually pure. To purify them, do this: Sprinkle purgation water on them; then have them shave their whole bodies and wash their clothes, and so purify themselves' (Num. 8.7). The priests, too, were inaugurated by rituals, including purification by water (Lev. 8.6). The Psalmist even hints at the use of *me niddah* for repentant sinners who plead, 'Purge me with hyssop [used to sprinkle *me niddah*] and I shall be pure' (Ps. 51.9; cf. also Ezek. 36.25).[13]

In conclusion, at Qumran the impurity of outsiders is primarily a label which enforces the barrier between member and non-member of the sect protecting the latter from physical harm and immoral influences as well as undesirable penetration by non-Israelites into the group. Hayes' conclusion with regard to other ancient Jewish groups is appropriate also for Qumran: 'Jewish ascriptions of impurity to Gentiles both constructed and reinforced the boundary needed to preserve group identity ... the fear of intergroup unions and their threat to group identity are the basis for ascriptions of impurity to outsiders' (Hayes 2002: 162). At Qumran, both Jewish and Gentile outsiders are considered impure, a term the sect uses to indicate both moral and ritual impurity. The differences between these two groups emerge only when they seek entrance to the sect. The Jewish novitiate is considered a full-fledged member after the entry process whereas the Gentile proselyte is not fully accepted nor completely assimilated into the group.

13. Cf. also the baptisms of John and Paul, who use purification by water in the context of atonement from sin. Baumgarten (1999a: 209) argues that John's baptism is like that of Qumran in that it is an effective means to atonement as long as it is preceded by repentance.

Further Reading

Alon, G.
1977 'Levitical Uncleanness of Gentiles', in *Jews, Judaism and the Classical World: Studies in Jewish History in the Times of the Second Temple and Talmud* (Jerusalem: Magnes Press): 146–89.

Büchler, A.
1926–27 'The Levitical Impurity of the Gentile in Palestine Before the Year 70', *JQR* 17:1–79.

Hayes, C.
1999 'Intermarriage and Impurity in Ancient Jewish Sources', *HTR* 92: 3–36.
2002 *Gentile Impurities and Jewish Identities: Intermarriage and Conversion from the Bible to the Talmud* (New York: Oxford University Press).

Klawans, J.
2000 *Impurity and Sin in Ancient Judaism* (Oxford and New York: Oxford University Press).

Milgrom, J.
1993 'The Concept of Impurity in Jubilees and the Temple Scroll', *RevQ* 16: 277–84.

Schiffman, L.H.
1997 'Non-Jews in the Dead Sea Scrolls', in *The Quest for Context and Meaning: Studies in Biblical Intertextuality in Honor of James A. Sanders*, eds. C.A. Evans and S. Talmon (Leiden: E.J. Brill): 153–71.
2000a 'Israel', in *Encyclopedia of the Dead Sea Scrolls*, I, eds. L.H. Schiffman and J.C. VanderKam (New York: Oxford University Press): 388–91.

Werman, C.
1997 'Jubilees 30: Building a Paradigm for the Ban on Intermarriage', *HTR* 90: 1–22.

CONCLUSION

This study has collected and analysed the extant data of Qumran on the subject of purity in an effort to discover fundamental principles of the sect as well as the particular details of each type of impurity. Part I was devoted to the underlying ideology repeatedly found in the Scrolls and to an analysis of each relevant source. It emerged that the Qumran Community held the most rigorous interpretation of Scripture's purity laws known in ancient Judaism in a time when purity was already at a premium. At every turn, the authors consistently champion expanded notions of holiness, purity and impurity. Sources of impurity are more in number and greater in potency than found elsewhere and require extensive purification. Food was especially guarded by the sect and liquids were seen as able to transfer impurity even against their natural flow.

The human condition is described as frail from both a moral and physical perspective, and this is brought into relief upon examination of purification requirements. Impurity is inevitable as it wells up by means of natural processes within human beings. Human inadequacy is forever in full view and requires God's grace for atonement as well as complex purification rituals. Nevertheless, the hope of the community lies not in the present wretched state of humanity but in messianic fulfilment and apocalyptic victory. At present, purity enables the group to receive ongoing revelation, and, in the future, purity will ignite God's holiness in military battle. Purity makes it possible for the holy angels to reside among the sectarians and aid them in their fight against evil.

The correlations of purity data found among the Scrolls support the notion that the Qumran texts are a corpus with a fairly consistent sectarian ideology. While they originated at different times and places, they were adopted by the community living at Qumran, and more often than not they turn out to be compatible. Repeated claims include the community's status as a holy house for Aaron or Israel, complaints against the laxity of Jewish outsiders in matters of purity and the cult, and the exclusion of impure and disabled persons from community activities. The status of the holy city is of keen importance, and more than one text forbids impurity to invade its premises. Outsiders were equated with non-Israel and considered threatening to the group's identity; ritual impurity was applied to them in an effort to maintain separation. Several texts emphasize that food must be kept pure from the time of harvest to the moment of consumption, and exclusion from the communal meal was used as a penalty for various infractions of sectarian law. Since impurity is such a potent force, more ablutions and purification time are required than a simple reading of Scripture demands. Even wood, stone and earth are susceptible to impurity. Thus, the Qumran documents are not unrelated fragments but they champion a certain sectarian ideology based on a stringent interpretation of Scripture.

In Part II the examination of the particular impurities discussed in the Scrolls confirmed the notion that the sect held to a rigorous interpretation of Scripture as well as to an ascetic lifestyle at Qumran. Comparison of the details of the Scrolls with Rabbinic *halakha* often clarified the issues and confirmed the relevance during the Second Temple period of concerns frequently labelled 'late' or 'Rabbinic.' Both groups forbid burial within walled cities, both are explicit that the leper is a sinner; both separate severely impure persons from other impure persons; both refer to the seclusion of women during menstruation; both are concerned to maintain the purity of food, in some cases, even from the time of harvest; and laws regarding the impurity of Gentiles are found in both sets of literature.

Nevertheless, there is a decided contrast between the sectarian character of the Scrolls as opposed to greater inclusion and flexibility among the Rabbis. The separatism of the Qumranites is demonstrated best in their willingness to abandon society and normal family life and move to the desert in anticipation of the eschaton. This stands in direct contrast to the Rabbinic emphasis on marriage and procreation. While the Rabbis could be harsh in their attitude towards the common people, they appear flexible when compared with the priestly ascetics of Qumran. Also, Rabbinic laws restricting women take on a better light when compared with the attitude towards women in the Scrolls. The sectarian authors not only exclude women from the Qumran Community but apparently from Jerusalem as well and severely constrain them even in ordinary cities. Some authors isolate women during menstruation and childbirth and forbid them to eat of the Passover sacrifice. Although excrement is not rendered impure in the Rabbinic impurity system, sectarian laws governing evacuation border on the impossible.

Finally, the biblical emphasis on the God of life and holiness as opposed to the forces of death and impurity is also reflected in the Dead Sea Scrolls. Several of the impurities of the Scrolls remind the authors of death. The leper, a sinner who is visibly decaying, gains hope when strengthened by the spirit of life. Sexual processes, celebrated by the Rabbis as a source of life, seem to be only a reminder of mortality and inherent impurity to the sectarians. It is also likely that the special water used to purify from corpse impurity was used to purify other impurities as well, including outsiders wishing to join the sect. Indeed, the sectarians regarded entry into their community as passing from darkness, impurity and death into light, purity and life.

Appendix A

PURITY CORRELATIONS IN THE QUMRAN SCROLLS

Purity Topic/Issue	References
Community	
The community is a holy house	1QS 8.5, 8; 9.6; 4Q174 3.6; 1Q28a 1.9; 1Q28b 4.27-28; 1QH 19[11].10-11; 1Q33 3.4; 6.6; cf. CD 20.2-7
Accusations against opponents' laxity	4Q171 1–2 i 19; CD 1.18-20; 4QMMT 3–94
Stages of acceptance to community based on purity	1QS 6.16-22; 7.20-23; CD 15.15; cf. *War* 2.138; 4Q265 1 ii 3-9
Exclusion of disabled and impure persons	1QM 7.4-6; 1Q28a 2.3-8; 1QH 11[3].21-22; 11Q19 45.7-18; cf. 4QMMT 51–57, 63
Food	
Harvesting and crushing fruit in purity	4Q284a 1.2-8; 2.2; 4Q274 3 i 6-9; 3 ii 7-9
Fourth-year holy fruit belongs to the priests	4Q396 1 iii 2-3; 11Q19 60.2-4; 4Q251 10.8-9; 4Q266 6 iv; 4Q270
Grain, wine and oil festivals desanctify crops	4Q251 9.1-6; 11Q19 43.3-10
Exclusion from the 'purity' used as a penalty	1QS 7.1-27; 8.17-24; 4Q267 18 iv 12-15; CD 9.21-23; 4Q265
Purification required before meals even for impure persons	1QS 5.13; 4Q514; cf. 4Q512 7–9 xi 1-4; 4Q274 2.1-2; 4Q513 1-2 ii 1; *War* 2.129
Contamination	
Even wood, stone and earth are susceptible to impurity	CD 12.15-17; 11Q19 49.12-16
Liquid transmits impurity	CD 12.15-17; 11Q19 49.11-12; cf. 4Q513 13.4-5
Purification	
Prohibition on shallow immersion pool	CD 10.11-13; 4Q513 13 i 1; 4Q270 10 iv 20
Ablutions required on the first day of impurity	11Q19 49.17; 50.14; 4Q414 2 ii 2; 4Q514 1 i 3-10; 4Q284; 4Q274 1.3-9
Purification rituals prohibited on Sabbath	4Q274 2 i 1-2; 4Q265 7.3-4; cf. 4Q251 1
Purification includes waiting for sunset on the last day of impurity	4Q267 9 ii 1–4; 4Q394 1 i 18–19; 4Q396 1 iv 1; 11Q19 50.12-16; 51.2-5; 4Q284 2–3

Purity Topic/Issue	References
Moral vs. Ritual Impurity	
Moral and ritual impurity are inherent in the human condition	1QH 5[13].21; 9 [1].22; 22 [18].4-5;1QS 11.9; cf. 4Q265 7
Ritual purification requires penitence/atonement	4Q512 29–32 vii 8-10, 18; 28.1-4; 99.2; 1QH 11[3].21; 4Q414 2 i 1-6; 4Q284; 4Q274 1 i 1; 1QS 3.7-9
Sin causes ritual as well as moral defilement	1QS 5.13-15, 20; cf. 6.24–25; 8.16-18
Purity enables participation with the angels	1QH 11[3].21-22; 19[11].13; 1QM 7.6; 1Q28a 2.8-9
Corpse/Carcass Impurity	
The foetus is a separate life; a dead foetus is a corpse	11Q19 50.10-13; 4Q270 9 ii 15-17; 4QMMT 39–41
Impurity of skins of animals not slaughtered within the holy city	4QMMT 21–36; 11Q19 47.7-18
Leprosy	
The leper is considered a sinner	4Q512 viii; 4QMMT B 73; 4Q270; 4Q267 9 i; 4Q266 2–3
Bodily Discharges	
Celibacy encouraged	CD 7.5-7; 1QS; cf. 11Q19 45.11-12
No sexual intercourse allowed in the holy city	CD 12.1-2; 11Q19 45.11-12
Impurity of excrement	4Q265 6.2; 11Q19 46.15; 4Q472a; cf. *War* 2.147-49
Outsiders	
Impurity of outsiders	1QS 3.4-5; 5.13-20; 1QH 13.21; 4Q284a 1.2-8
Impurity of Gentiles	4Q266 5 ii 5-7; 4Q267 6 ii 5-9; 1Q19 63.15 1QS 5.4; 4Q514; 4Q251 16.2-3; cf. *War* 2.150; Acts 10.38
Forbidden spouses of priests not allowed to eat priestly food	4Q251 16.2-3; 4Q513 1–2 ii 1-5; cf. 4QMMT 81–91

Appendix B

A COMPARISON OF THE IMPURITY LAWS OF THE BIBLE, QUMRAN AND THE RABBIS

Bible	Qumran	Rabbis
Corpse		
No burial within the camp, Num. 5.2	No burial within walled cities, 11Q19 48.11-14	No burial within walled cities, m. *Kel.* 1.7
The contents of the tent of death is impure, Num. 19.18	The house and its contents, even stone, become impure, 11Q19 49.5-7, 11-16; CD 12.15-18	The house of death itself does not become impure, only persons and complete, usable vessels within it. Stone, earth and dung are not susceptible to impurity, m. *Kel.* 2.1; 11.2; m. *Oh.* 5.5; *Sif. Num.* 126[162]
Corpse-impure persons purify on the third and seventh days of their impurity, Num. 31.19	Corpse-impure persons purify on the first, third and seventh days of their impurity,11Q19 49.13-17	Corpse-impure persons purify on the third and seventh days of their impurity. The mourner is forbidden to bathe, m. *MQ* 15b
Corpse-impure persons are barred from the camp, Num. 5.2	Corpse-impure persons are barred from the holy city and sequestered within ordinary cities, 11Q19 45.17; 49.20-21	Corpse-impure persons are barred from the Temple but not from Jerusalem, m. *Kel.* 1.6-9
The contents of an open vessel in the house of death become impure, Num. 19.15	Even the contents of a sealed vessel will be impure for the 'pure man', 11Q19 49.8; 4Q274 3 ii	The contents of a sealed vessel in the house of death are protected; in fact, earthenware only receives impurity through its interior, *Sif. shem. sher. par.* 7.5; *Sif. meṣ. zab. par.* 3.2
The corpse-impure person must be sprinkled with purgation water by a pure person, Num. 19.17-18	Only a mature priest can sprinkle the purgation water on the impure, 4Q277 1 ii 6-7	The Mishnah implies that young boys were elected to sprinkle the purgation water, m. *Par.* 3.2-4

Bible	Qumran	Rabbis
Carcass		
Touching a carcass makes a person impure, and carrying the carcass requires laundering, Lev. 11.39-40	Touching or carrying a carcass including its skin, flesh and claws, causes impurity and requires bathing and laundering, 11Q19 51.1-5	Touching or carrying the flesh of a carcass causes impurity; hides, horns and hooves do not convey impurity by touch, m. *Ḥul.* 9.1, 5; m. *Toh.* 1.4; m. *Zab.* 5.3
All slaughter of domestic animals has to be sacrificial, Lev. 17.3	Food or drink cannot be brought into the Temple City in skins of non-ritually slaughtered animals, 11Q19 47.7-18	The hide of a carcass does not convey impurity by touch, m. *Toh.* 1.4, m. *Ḥul.* 9.1
Leprosy		
The leper is considered a sinner, Num. 12.9-10; 2 Kgs 5.27; 2 Sam. 3.29; Lev. 26.21; Deut. 28.27; Job 22.5	The leper is considered a sinner, 4Q512 viii; 4QMMT B 73; 4Q270; 4Q267 9 i; 4Q266 2–3	The leper is considered a sinner, t. *Neg.* 6.7; *Sif. meṣ. neg. par.* 5.7-9; b. *Ar.* 15b-16a; *Lev. R.* 17.3.
The priest examines and pronounces the leper impure, Lev. 13.3	The overseer of the community may instruct the priest who pronounces the leper impure, CD 13.5-6	An ignorant priest may be instructed by a sage before pronouncing the leper impure, m. *Neg.* 3.1; 4.7-10; *Sif. meṣ. neg.* 1.1
The leper must dwell outside the camp, Num. 5.2	Installations are provided for the leper outside of all cities, 11Q19 46.16-18; 48.14-17	Lepers are excluded from all walled cities, m. *Kel.* 1.7
The leper dwells alone and cries 'impure, impure' to passers-by, Lev. 13.46; Num. 5.2	Lepers and other severely impure persons dwell alone lest they contaminate even other impure persons; 'impure, impure' means 'impure to the impure', 4Q274	Lepers may not live with other types of impure persons. 'Impure, impure' means 'impure to the impure' *Sif. taz. neg.* 12.12-13; b. *Ar.* 16b; b. *Pes.* 67a; cf. *Ant.* 3.264; *Ag. Ap.* 1.281
Lepers do not become pure until sacrifices are offered on the eighth day of purification, Lev. 14.10-11	Lepers must offer sacrifices on the eighth day of purification but do not become pure until evening, 4QMMT 71–72	Lepers become pure after sacrifices are offered on the eighth day of purification, b. *Yoma* 16a, 30b

Bible	Qumran	Rabbis
Flux		
Persons with flux are put out of the camp, Num. 5.2	Areas are allotted to the east of the Temple City and within ordinary cities for those with flux,11Q19 48.14-18; 4Q2741 i 4-5	Persons with flux are excluded from the Temple Mount; m. *Kel.* 1.3; m. *Zab.* 5.6-7; women with flux may have been quarantined, m. *Nid.* 7.4; *ARN A* 2.3; *Targ. Ps-Jon.* on Lev. 12.2; cf. *Ant.* 3.261
The bed and seat of a person with flux contaminate those who touch them, Lev. 15.5-6	Objects which the person with flux touches become secondarily contaminating to other persons, 4Q274 1 i 4-5	Only objects made for sitting/lying, on which the person with flux has applied his greater weight, will transmit impurity to a person, m. *Zab.* 2.4; 5.6
A *zabah* is a woman who has had abnormal menstruation for 'many days', Lev. 15.25	A *zabah* is a woman who has had any menstrual bleeding outside of her normal period, 4Q266 6 ii 2-4; 4Q267 9 ii 4	A *zabah* is a woman who has had abnormal menstruation for at least three successive days, *Sif. meṣ. zab. par.* 5.9
Childbirth		
New mother is contagious like a menstruant for seven or fourteen days depending on the gender of her child, after which she remains an impurity threat only to sancta for 33/66 days, Lev. 12.2-6	Apparently, the new mother is ritually contagious for the whole 40/80 days since she may not nurse her own baby, 4Q266 6 ii 11	The Rabbis consider the new mother ritually contagious only for 7/14 days and then she is only an impurity threat to sancta for the next 33/66 days (depending on the gender of the child), m. *Nid.* 4.6; 10.6
Graves and other containers of dead bodies convey contamination, Lev. 11.33; Num. 19.14ff	A dead foetus within a mother renders her impure as a grave, 11Q19 50.10-19	A dead foetus does not convey impurity until it emerges from its mother, m. *Ḥul.* 4.3
Menstruation		
Pure women are allowed to enter the court of the sanctuary, and even to present sacrifices, Lev. 12.6; 15.29	No women allowed to live in the Temple City since no installations for impurity are provided and sexual intercourse is forbidden, 11Q19 45.7-10; CD 12.1-2	Women are allowed to live in Jerusalem and worship at the Temple in the Court of the Women, m. *Kel.* 1.8; b. *Yoma* 16a

Bible	Qumran	Rabbis
No statement on isolation of the menstruant is prescribed in Scripture.	Women are to be isolated in ordinary cities during menstruation, 11Q19 48.13–17; cf. 4Q274 1 i 4-6	Women were possibly secluded during menstruation (m. *Nid.* 7.4, *Targ. Ps-Jon.* on Lev. 12.2; *ARN A* 2.3; cf. *Ant.* 3.261)
It is assumed that the menstruant must bathe after her week of impurity since even those who touch her must bathe, Lev. 15.19	The menstruant must bathe and launder her clothes after her week of impurity, 4Q514 5-6	The menstruant must bathe after her week of impurity, m. *Miq.* 8.1, 5
Passover sacrifice was eaten by families, Ex. 12.3	Women are not allowed to eat of the Passover sacrifice, 4Q265 3; 11Q19 17.8-9	Women are allowed to eat the Passover sacrifice if they are free from impurity, m. *Pes.* 8.1; cf. *War* 6.426
Semen		
Sexual relations are prohibited only in sacred contexts, cf. Ex. 19.10-11	The Qumran Community is celibate; no sexual intercourse is allowed in the Temple City, 11Q19 46.16-18; CD 12.1-2	Although sexual relations are not allowed at the Temple, marriage is a holy obligation and sexual relations are encouraged, b. *Yoma* 72b; b. *Pes.* 112b, b. *Men.* 110b, b. *Ta'an.* 16a; b. *Qid.* 29b
Those who emit semen are required to bathe and launder their clothes but they are not sent out of the city, Lev. 15.16-17	Those who emit semen are sequestered outside of the Temple City for three days and must perform ablutions on days one and three, 11Q19 45.7-10	Those who emit semen are required to perform ablutions and then they will not convey impurity as long as they do not touch sancta until sunset, cf. m. *TY* 2.2f; *Sif. shem. sher.* 8.9
Only those persons or objects directly in contact with semen become impure, Lev. 15.17	Touching or carrying any object which contains semen causes defilement, 4Q274 2 i 8	Semen does not defile except by direct contact, b. *Naz.* 66a; m. *Zab.* 5.11; *Sif. meṣ. zab.* 2.8

Bible	Qumran	Rabbis
Excrement		
Although excrement is not discussed in the ritual impurities of Lev. 11–15, is not allowed to defecation within the holy War Camp, Dt. 23.12-13; cf. also Ezek. 4.14	No latrines are allowed within the Temple City but must be located 4500 feet NW of it, 11Q19 46.15; cf. 4Q265 6.2; 7 i 3; 4Q472; cf. *War* 2.147-49	Latrines should be set up in every city, b. *San.* 17b
No proscription on defecation on the Sabbath is recorded, but it is not allowed in the holy War Camp, Dt. 23.12-13	Excrement impurity is not allowed on the Sabbath; 11Q19 46.15; cf. 4Q265 6.2; 7 i 3; *War* 2.147-49	Excrement does not ritually defile, m. *TY* 2.1; m. *Makh.* 6.7; t. *Miq.* 7.8; y. *Pes.* 7.11, 35b
Outsiders		
Sin is labelled impure and sinners are associated with impurity, Lev. 18.24-30; 19.31; 20.1-3; Num. 35.33-34; Isa. 52.1; 35.8; Jl. 3.17 (Eng.); Zech. 14.21; Ezek. 36.17	Outsiders are ritually defiling, 1QS 3.4–5; 5.13-20; 4Q284a 1.2–8; 11Q19 63.15; 4Q266 5 ii 5-7	Conflicting views exist as to whether or not Gentiles are ritually defiling, cf. Chapter 6
Food		
Wet produce is susceptible to impurity, Lev. 11.38	Fruit must be harvested in a state of purity, 4Q284a 1.4; 4Q274 3 ii 7-9	Certain fruit, e.g. olives, grapes, must be harvested in purity, m. *Toh.* 9-10
Fourth-year fruit is holy, Lev. 19.24	Fourth-year fruit belongs to the priests, 4QMMT 62-63; 11Q19 60.2-4; 4Q251 15-16; 4Q266 6 iv; 4Q270	Fourth year fruit is eaten in Jerusalem by its owners, *Ma*ʿ*as. Sh* 5.2, 11-12
Food purity laws are addressed to all Israel, Lev. 11.1; priests maintain purity before eating holy food, Lev. 7.20	Purification required even of hopelessly impure persons before meals, 4Q514; 4Q512 xi 9; 1QS 5.13; 4Q274 2.1; 4Q514 1.4; cf. *War* 2.129	General assumption that ordinary food should be eaten in purity. m. *Ḥul.* 2.5; m. *Zab.* 3.2; t. *Miq.* 6.

Bibliography

Albeck, Ch.

1953 *Shisha Sidrei Mishnah*, VI (Jerusalem: Bialik Institute).

Alon, G.

1977 'Levitical Uncleanness of Gentiles', in *Jews, Judaism and the Classical World: Studies in Jewish History in the Times of the Second Temple and Talmud* (Jerusalem: Magnes Press): 146–89.

Attridge, H.W. and R.A. Oden (eds.)

1976 *De Dea Syria attributed to Lucian* (Missoula, MT: Scholars Press).

Baillet M.

1962 *Les 'petites grottes' de Qumrân Grotte, Discoveries in the Judaean Desert*, III, (Oxford: Clarendon Press).

1982 *Qumran Grotte 4.[3]III (4Q482–4Q520), Discoveries in the Judaean Desert*, VII (Oxford: Clarendon Press).

Baumgarten, J.M.

1967 'The Essene Avoidance of Oil and the Laws of Purity', *RevQ* 6: 183–93.

1976 '4Q Halakha, the Law of Hadash, and the Pentecontad Calendar', *JJS* 27/1: 36–46.

1977 *Studies in Qumran Law* (Leiden: E.J. Brill).

1990 'The Qumran-Essene Restraints on Marriage', in *Archaeology and History in the Dead Sea Scrolls*, ed. L.H. Schiffman (Sheffield: JSOT Press): 13–24.

1992a 'The Disqualifications of Priests in 4Q Fragments of the "Damascus Document", a Specimen of the Recovery of Pre-Rabbinic Halakha', in *The Madrid Qumran Congress*, II; STDJ 11; (eds. J. Trebolle-Barrera and L.V. Montaner; Leiden: E.J. Brill): 503–13.

1992b 'The Purification Rituals of DJD 7', *The Dead Sea Scrolls: Forty Years of Research*, eds. D. Dimant and U. Rappaport (Leiden: E.J. Brill): 199–209.

1994a 'Liquids and Susceptibility to Defilement in New 4Q Texts', in *The Community of the Renewed Covenant*, eds. E. Ulrich and J.C. VanderKam (Notre Dame, IN: University of Notre Dame Press): 91–101.

1994b '*Zab* Impurity in Qumran and Rabbinic Law', *JJS* 45: 273–78.

1995a 'A Fragment on Fetal Life and Pregnancy in 4Q270', in *Pomegranates and Golden Bells*, ed. D. Wright (Winona Lake, IN: Eisenbrauns): 445–48.

1995b 'The Red Cow Purification Rites in Qumran Texts', *JJS* 46: 112–19.

1996 *Qumran Cave Four XIII: The Damascus Document (4Q266–273), Discoveries in the Judaean Desert, XVIII* (Oxford: Clarendon Press).

1999a 'The Purification Liturgies', in *The Dead Sea Scrolls after Fifty Years*, II, eds. P. Flint and J.C. Vanderkam (Leiden: E.J. Brill): 202–12.

1999b *Qumran Cave 4 XXV: Halakhic Texts, Discoveries in the Judaean Desert XXXV* (Oxford: Clarendon Press).

2000 'Damascus Document', *Encyclopedia of the Dead Sea Scrolls*, I, eds. L.H. Schiffman and J.C. VanderKam (New York: Oxford University Press): 166–70.

Biale, R.

1995 *Women and Jewish Law: An Exploration of Women's Issues in Halakhic Sources* (New York: Schocken Books).

Boyarin, D.

1993 *Carnal Israel: Reading Sex in Talmudic Culture* (Berkeley: University of California Press).

Brooke, G.

2000 'Florilegium', in *Encyclopedia of the Dead Sea Scrolls*, I, eds. L.H. Schiffman and J.C. VanderKam (New York: Oxford University Press): 297–98.

Broshi, M.

1992 'Anti-Qumranic Polemics in the Talmud', in *The Madrid Congress: Proceedings of the International Congress on the Dead Sea Scrolls*, II, eds. J. Trebolle-Barrera and L.V. Montaner (Leiden: E.J. Brill): 589–600.

Büchler, A.

1926–27 'The Levitical Impurity of the Gentile in Palestine Before the Year 70', *JQR* 17: 1–79.

Cohen, S.

1999 'Purity, Piety, and Polemic: Medieval Rabbinic Denunciations of "Incorrect" Purification Practices', in *Women and Water: Menstruation in Jewish Life and Law*, ed. R. Wasserfall (Waltham, MA: Brandeis University Press): 82–100.

Collins, J.J.

1999 'In the Likeness of the Holy Ones: The Creation of Humankind in a Wisdom Text from Qumran', in *The Provo International Conference on the Dead Sea Scrolls*, eds. D. Parry and E. Ulrich (Leiden: E.J. Brill): 609–18.

Cook, L.A.

1999 'Body Language: Women's Rituals of Purification in the Bible and Mishnah', in *Women and Water: Menstruation in Jewish Life and Law*, ed. Rahel Wasserfall (Waltham, MA: Brandeis University Press): 40–59.

Cross, F.

1994 'Appendix: Paleographical Dates of the Manuscripts', in *The Dead Sea Scrolls: Hebrew, Aramaic, and Greek Texts with English Translations. Vol. 1: Rule of the Community and Related Documents*, ed. J.H. Charlesworth (Tübingen: J.C.B. Mohr [Paul Siebeck]; Louiseville, KY: Westminster/ John Knox Press): 57.

Davidson, M.J.

1992 *Angels at Qumran: A Comparative Study of 1 Enoch 1–36, 72–108 and Sectarian Writings from Qumran* (Sheffield: JSOT Press).

Davies, P.R.
2000 'War of the Sons of Light against the Sons of Darkness', in *Encylopedia of the Dead Sea Scrolls*, II, ed. L.H. Schiffman (Oxford: Oxford University Press): 965–68.

Dimant, D.
1986 '*4QFlorilegium* and the Idea of the Community as Temple', in *Hellenica et Judaica: Hommage à Valentin Nikiprowetzky*, ed. A. Caquot *et al.* (Leuven-Paris: Editions Peeters): 165–89.

Douglas, M.
1966 *Purity and Danger* (London: Routledge Press).
1975 *Implicit Meanings: Essays in Anthropology* (London: Routledge & Kegan Paul).
1982 *Natural Symbols: Explorations in Cosmology* (New York: Pantheon Books).
1985 'The Abominations of Leviticus', in *Anthropological Approaches to the Old Testament*, ed. B. Lang (Philadelphia: Fortress Press): 100–116.
1993 *In the Wilderness: The Doctrine of Defilement in the Book of Numbers* (Sheffield: Sheffield Academic Press).

Durkheim, E.
1915 *The Elementary Forms of the Religious Life* (London: G. Allen & Unwin).

Eilberg-Schwartz, H.
1992 *People of the Body: Jews and Judaism from an Embodied Perspective* (Albany, NY: State University of New York Press).

Elgvin, T.
1999 '472a. 4QHalakha C', in *Qumran Cave 4 XXV: Halakhic Texts, Discoveries in the Judaean Desert XXXV* (Oxford: Clarendon Press): 155–56.

Eliade, M.
1959 *The Sacred and the Profane: The Nature of Religion*, tr. W. Trask (New York: Harcourt, Brace & World).

Eshel, E.
1997 '4Q414 Fragment 2: Purification of a Corpse-Contaminated Person', in *Legal Texts and Legal Issues: The Proceedings of the Second Meeting of the International Organization for Qumran Studies, Published in Honor of Joseph M. Baumgarten* (Leiden: E.J. Brill): 3–10.
1999 'Ritual of Purification', in *Qumran Cave 4 XXV: Halakhic Texts, Discoveries in the Judaean Desert XXXV* (Oxford: Clarendon Press): 135–54.

Eshel, H.
2000 'CD 12:15–17 and the Stone Vessels found at Qumran', in *The Damascus Document: A Centennial of Discovery*, ed. J.M. Baumgarten *et al.* (Leiden: E.J. Brill): 45–52.

Frymer-Kensky, T.
1983 'Pollution, Purification, and Purgation in Biblical Israel', in *The Word of the Lord Shall Go Forth: Essays in Honor of David Noel Freedman in Celebration of His Sixtieth Birthday*, eds. Carol L. Meyers and M. O'Connor (Winona Lake, IN: Eisenbrauns): 399–414.

García Martínez, F.
1999 'Les Limites de la Communauté: Pureté et Impureté à Qumrân et dans le Nouveau Testament', in *Text and Testimony*, (Kampen, Netherlands: J.H. Kok): 111–22.
1996 '4QMMT in a Qumran Context', *Reading MMT: Essays in Honor of A.F.J. Klijn*, ed. T. Boarde *et al. New Perspectives on Qumran Law and History*, eds. M. Bernstein and J. Kampen (Atlanta: Scholars Press):15–27.
2000 'Temple Scroll', in *Encyclopedia of the Dead Sea Scrolls*, II, eds. L.H. Schiffman and J.C. VanderKam (New York: Oxford University Press): 927–33.
García Martínez, F. and J. Trebolle-Barrera
1995 *The People of the Dead Sea Scrolls* (Leiden: E.J. Brill).

Geiger, A.
1928 *Ha-Mikra ve-Targumav* (Jerusalem: Mossad Bialik).
Ginzberg, L.
1976 *An Unknown Jewish Sect* (New York: Jewish Theological Seminary Press).
Gray, G.B.
1903 *A Critical and Exegetical Commentary on Numbers*, International Critical Commentary (New York: C. Scribner's Sons).
Greenberg, M.
1995 'The Etymology of *Niddah* (Heb.) "(Menstrual) Impurity"', in *Solving Riddles and Untying Knots* (Winona Lake, IN: Eisenbrauns): 69–77.
Hachlili, R.
1979 'Ancient Burial Customs Preserved in Jericho Hills', *BAR* 5/4.
2000 'Cemeteries', in *Encyclopedia of the Dead Sea Scrolls*, I, eds. L.H. Schiffman and J.C. VanderKam (Oxford: Oxford University Press): 125–29.
Hachlili, R. and A. Killebrew
1983 'Jewish Funerary Customs during the Second Temple Period in Light of the Excavations at the Jericho Necropolis', *PEQ* 115: 109–39.
Halevi, I.
1967 *Dorot ha-Rishonim*, I–VI (Jerusalem).
Harrington, H.
1993 *The Impurity Systems of the Rabbis and Qumran* (Atlanta: Scholars Press).
1995 'Did the Pharisees Eat Ordinary Food in a State of Purity?', *JStJud* 26: 42–54.
2001 *Holiness: Rabbinic Judaism and the Graeco-Roman World* (London: Routledge Press).
Hauck, F. *et al.*
1964–76 '*Katharos*' in *Theological Dictionary of the New Testament*, III, ed. G.W. Bromley (Grand Rapids, MI: Eerdmans): 413–31.
Hayes, C.
1999 'Intermarriage and Impurity in Ancient Jewish Sources', *HTR* 92: 3–36.
2002 *Gentile Impurities and Jewish Identities: Intermarriage and Conversion from the Bible to the Talmud* (New York: Oxford University Press).

Hengel, M.
1974 *Judaism and Hellenism* (Philadelphia: Fortress Press).
Himmelfarb, M.
2001 'Impurity and Sin in 4QD, 1QS, and 4Q512', *DSD* 8/1: 9–37.
Hubner, H.
1992 'Unclean and Clean (NT)', in *Anchor Bible Dictionary*, VI, ed. D.N. Freedman (New York: Doubleday): 741–45.
Klawans, J.
1998 'Idolatry, Incest, and Impurity: Moral Defilement in Ancient Judaism', *JStJud* 29/4: 391–415.
2000 *Impurity and Sin in Ancient Judaism* (Oxford and New York: Oxford University Press).
Knibb, M.
2000 'Rule of the Community's in *Encyclopedia of the Dead Sea Scrolls*, II, eds. L.H. Schiffman and J.C. VanderKam (New York: Oxford University Press): 793–97.
Kon, M.
1947 *The Tombs of the Kings* (Hebrew) (Tel Aviv: Dvir): 31–38.
Leach, E.
1976 *Culture and Communication: The Logic by which symbols are Connected* (Cambridge: Cambridge University Press).
Levine, B.
1993 *Numbers 1–20*, Anchor Bible 4 (New York: Doubleday): 463–64.
Licht, J.
1965a *Megillat Ha-Serakhim* (Jerusalem: Bialik Institute).
1965b '*Qodesh, Qadosh, Qedushah*', in *Entsiqlopedya Mikra'it*, VII, eds. E. Sukenik and M.D. Cassuto (Jerusalem: Bialik Institute): 44–62.
Lieberman, S.
1952 'The Discipline in the So-Called Dead Sea Manual of Discipline', *JBL* 71: 199–206.
Maccoby, H.
1999 *Ritual and Morality: The Ritual Purity System and Its Place in Judaism* (Cambridge: Cambridge University Press).
Magen, Y.
1988 *The Stone Vessel Industry in Jerusalem during the Second Temple Period* (Heb.) (Jerusalem: Society for the Preservation of Nature).
Magness, J.
2000 'A Reassessment of the Excavations of Qumran', in *The Dead Sea Scrolls Fifty Years after Their Discovery 1947–1997*, ed. L. Schiffman *et al.* (Jerusalem: Israel Exploration Society): 708–19.
Maimonides, M.
1954 'The Book of Cleanness', in *Code of Maimonides*, X, tr. H. Danby, Yale Judaica Series, VIII (New Haven, CT: Yale University Press).
Malina, B.J.
1981 *The New Testament World: Insights from Cultural Anthropology* (Atlanta: John Knox Press).

Mazar, A.
1975 'The Aqueducts of Jerusalem', in *Jerusalem Revealed: Archaeology in the Holy City 1968–1974*, ed. Y. Yadin (Jerusalem: Israel Exploration Society).

Meacham, T.
1999 'An Abbreviated History of the Development of the Jewish Menstrual Laws', in *Women and Water: Menstruation in Jewish Life and Law*, ed. R. Wasserfall (Waltham, MA: Brandeis University Press): 23-39.

Milgrom, J.
1981 'The Paradox of the Red Cow (Num. XIX)', *Vetus Testamentum* 31: 62-72.
1982 'Religious Conversion and the Revolt Model for the Formation of Israel', *JBL* 101: 169-76.
1989a 'The Qumran Cult: Its Exegetical Principles', in *Temple Scroll Studies*, ed. G.J. Brooke (Sheffield: JSOT Press): 165-80.
1989b 'Rationale for Cultic Law: The Case of Impurity', *Semeia* 45: 103-109.
1990a 'Ethics and Ritual: The Foundations of the Biblical Dietary Laws', in *Religion and Law: Biblical, Judaic and Islamic Perspectives*, ed. E.B. Firmage *et al.* (Winona Lake: Eisenbrauns): 159–91.
1990b 'The Scriptural Foundations and Deviations in the Laws of Purity of the Temple Scroll', in *Archaeology and History in the Dead Sea Scrolls*, ed. L.H. Schiffman (Sheffield: JSOT Press): 83–99.
1991 *Leviticus1–16*, The Anchor Bible 3A (Garden City, NY: Doubleday).
1993 'The Concept of Impurity in Jubilees and the Temple Scroll', *RevQ* 16: 277–84.
1994a 'The Purification Rule', in *The Dead Sea Scrolls: Hebrew, Aramaic, and Greek Texts with English Translations*, I, *Rule of the Community and Related Documents*, ed. J.H. Charlesworth (Tübingen: J.C.B. Mohr [Paul Siebeck]; Louisville, KY: Westminster/John Knox Press): 177–79.
1994b '4QTOHOROT[a]: An Unpublished Qumran Text on Purities', in *Time to Prepare the Way in the Wilderness: Papers on the Qumran Scrolls*, eds. D. Dimant and L.H. Schiffman (Leiden: E.J. Brill): 59–68.
2000 *Leviticus 17–22*, The Anchor Bible 3A (Garden City, NY: Doubleday).

Naude, J.
1999 'Holiness in the Dead Sea Scrolls', in *The Dead Sea Scrolls after Fifty Years*, II, ed. P.W. Flint and J.C. VanderKam (Leiden: E.J. Brill): 171–99.

Neusner, J.
1976 *History of the Mishnaic Law of Purities*, I (Leiden: E. J. Brill).
1994 *Purity in Rabbinic Judaism* (Atlanta: Scholars Press).

Newton, M.
1985 *The Concept of Purity at Qumran and in the Letters of Paul* (Cambridge: Cambridge University Press).

Nitzan, B.
1986 *Megillat Pesher Habakkuk* (Jerusalem).

Oepke, A.
1964 '*Bapto*', in *Theological Dictionary of the New Testament*, I, ed. G.W. Bromley (Grand Rapids, MI: Eerdmans): 529–46.
Parker, R.
1983 *Miasma: Pollution and Purification in Early Greek Religion* (Oxford: Clarendon Press).
Pfann, S.
1999 'Midrash Sefer Moshe', in *Qumran Cave 4 XXV: Halakhic Texts, Discoveries in the Judaean Desert XXXV*, ed. J.M. Baumgarten (Oxford: Clarendon Press): 1–24.
Qimron, E.
1988 'The Holiness of the Holy Land in the Light of a New Document from Qumran', in *The Holy Land in History and Thought*, ed. M. Sharon (Leiden: E.J. Brill): 9–13.
1991 'Notes on the 4Q Zadokite Fragment on Skin Disease', *JJS* 42/2: 256–59.
1992 'Celibacy in the Dead Sea Scrolls and the Two Kinds of Sectarians', in *The Madrid Qumran Congress: Proceedings of the International Congress on the Dead Sea Scrolls, Madrid, 18–21, March 1991*, I, eds. J. Trebolle-Barrera and L.V. Montaner (Leiden: E.J. Brill): 287–94.
Qimron, E. and J.H. Charlesworth
1994 'Rule of the Community', in *The Dead Sea Scrolls: Hebrew, Aramaic, and Greek Texts with English Translations. Vol. 1: Rule of the Community and Related Documents*, eds. J.H. Charlesworth (Tübingen: J.C.B. Mohr [Paul Siebeck]; Louisville, KY: Westminster/John Knox Press): 1–5.
Qimron, E. and J. Strugnell.
1994 *Qumran Cave 4 V: Miqsat Ma'ase ha-Torah*, DJD X (Oxford: Clarendon Press).
Rabinowitz, L.I.
1971 'Leprosy', in *Encyclopedia Judaica*, XI (Jerusalem: Keter): 33–39.
Regev, E.
2000a 'Non-Priestly Purity and Its Religious Aspects according to Historical Sources and Archaeological Findings', in *Purity and Holiness*, ed. M. Poorthuis (Leiden: E.J. Brill): 223–44.
2000b 'Pure Individualism: The Idea of Non-Priestly Purity in Ancient Judaism', *JStJud* 31/2: 176–202.
Reich, R.
1980 'Mishnah Sheqalim 8:2 and the Archaeological Evidence', in *Jerusalem in the Second Temple Period: Abraham Schalit Memorial Volume*, eds. A. Oppenheimer, U. Rappaport and M. Stern (Jerusalem: Yad Izhak Ben-Zvi and Ministry of Defence).
1987 'Synagogue and Ritual Bath during the Second Temple and the Period of the Mishna and Talmud', in *Synagogues in Antiquity*, ed. M. Kasher *et al.* (Jerusalem): 205–12.
2000 '*Miqwa'ot* at Khirbet Qumran and the Jerusalem Connection', in *The Dead Sea Scrolls Fifty Years after Their Discovery 1947–1997*, ed. L. Schiffman *et al.* (Jerusalem: Israel Exploration Society): 728–31.

Ringgren, H.
1986 '*Tahar*', in *Theological Dictionary of the Old Testament*, V, eds. G. J. Botterweck and H. Ringgren, tr. D. Green (Grand Rapids, MI: Eerdmans): 287–96.

Rosovsky, N.
1992 'A Thousand Years of History in Jerusalem's Jewish Quarter', *BAR* 18/3: 31.

Sacchi, P.
1979 'Da Qohelet al tempo di Gesu', in *Aufstieg und Niedergang der Romischen Welt*, II (Berlin and New York): 3–32.

Sanders, E.P.
1990 *Jewish Law from Jesus to the Mishnah* (London and Philadelphia: SCM and Trinity).

Schiffman, L.H.
1983a 'Legislation concerning Relations with Non-Jews in the Zadokite Fragments and in Tannaitic Literature, *RevQ* 11:43, 385–87.
1983b *Sectarian Law in the Dead Sea Scrolls: Courts, Testimony and the Penal Code* (Chico, CA: Scholars Press).
1990a 'The Impurity of the Dead in the Temple Scroll', in *Archaeology and History in the Dead Sea Scrolls*, ed. L.H. Schiffman, (Sheffield: JSOT Press): 135–56.
1990b 'Miqsat Ma'aseh ha-Torah and the Temple Scroll', *RevQ* 14: 435–57.
1992 'Laws Pertaining to Women in the Temple Scroll', in *The Dead Sea Scrolls: Forty Years of Research*, eds. D. Dimant and U. Rappaport (Leiden: E.J. Brill): 210–28.
1994a 'Ordinances and Rules' and 'Sectarian Rule 5Q13', in *The Dead Sea Scrolls: Hebrew, Aramaic, and Greek Texts with English Translations. Vol. 1: Rule of the Community and Related Documents*, ed. J.H. Charlesworth (Tübingen: J.C.B. Mohr [Paul Siebeck]; Louisville, KY: Westminster/ John Knox Press): 132–75.
1994b 'The Temple Scroll and the Nature of Its Law: The Status of the Question', in *The Community of the Renewed Covenant*, eds. E. Ulrich and J.C. VanderKam (Notre Dame, IN: University of Notre Dame Press): 37–55.
1996 'The Place of 4QMMT in the Corpus of Qumran Manuscripts', in *Reading MMT: New Perspectives on Qumran Law and History*, eds. M. Bernstein and J. Kampen (Atlanta: Scholars Press): 81–98.
1997 'Non-Jews in the Dead Sea Scrolls', in *The Quest for Context and Meaning: Studies in Biblical Intertextuality in Honor of James A. Sanders*, eds. C.A. Evans and S. Talmon (Leiden: E.J. Brill): 153–71.
2000a 'Israel', in *Encyclopedia of the Dead Sea Scrolls*, I, eds. L.H. Schiffman and J.C. VanderKam (New York: Oxford University Press): 388–91.
2000b 'Miqtsat Ma'asei ha-Torah', in *Encyclopedia of the Dead Sea Scrolls*, I, eds. L.H. Schiffman and J.C. VanderKam (New York: Oxford University Press): 558–60.
2000c 'Rule of the Congregation', in *Encyclopedia of the Dead Sea Scrolls*, II, eds.

L.H. Schiffman and J.C. VanderKam (New York: Oxford University Press): 797–99.

Schramm, G.
1992 'Meal Customs (Jewish)', in *Anchor Bible Dictionary*, IV (New York: Doubleday): 648–50.

Schwartz, D.R.
1990 'On Two Aspects of a Priestly View of Descent at Qumran', in *Archaeology and History in the Dead Sea Scrolls*, ed. L.H. Schiffman, (Sheffield: JSOT Press): 157–79.
1992 'Law and Truth: On Qumran-Sadducean and Rabbinic Views of Law', in *The Dead Sea Scrolls: Forty Years of Research*, eds. D. Dimant and U. Rappaport (Leiden: E.J. Brill): 229–40.
1996 'MMT, Josephus and the Pharisees', *Reading MMT: New Perspectives on Qumran Law and History*, eds. M. Bernstein and J. Kampen (Atlanta: Scholars Press): 67–80.

Schweid, E.
1971 '*Kedushah*', in *Encyclopedia Judaica*, X (Jerusalem: Keter): 866–75.

Spiro, S.
1980 'Who was the Chaber: A New Approach to an Ancient Institution?', *JStJud* 11/2: 186–216.

Talmon, S.
1994 'The Community of the Renewed Covenant: Between Judaism and Christianity', in *The Community of the Renewed Covenant*, eds. E. Ulrich and J.C. VanderKam (Notre Dame, IN: University of Notre Dame Press): 3–24.

Taylor, J.
1997 *The Immerser: John the Baptist within Second Temple Judaism* (Grand Rapids: Eerdmans).

Wacholder, B.Z.
1983 *The Dawn of Qumran: The Sectarian Torah and the Teacher of Righteousness* (Cincinatti: Hebrew Union College Press).
1989 'Rules of Testimony in Qumran Jurisprudence: CD 9 and 11QTorah 64', *JJS* 40: 163–74.

Weiss, I.H.
1904 *Dor, Dor v'Dor Shav*, I (Vilna).

Werman, C.
1997 'Jubilees 30: Building a Paradigm for the Ban on Intermarriage', *HTR* 90: 1–22.
2000 'The Concept of Holiness and the Requirements of Purity in Second Temple and Tannaitic Literature', in *Purity and Holiness*, ed. M. Poorthuis (Leiden: E.J. Brill).

Wilkinson, J.
1977 'Leprosy and Leviticus: The Problem of Description and Identification', *Scot J Th* 30: 153–69.

Wold, D.
1979 'The *Kareth* Penalty in P: Rationale and Cases', *SBL Seminar Papers* 1: 18.

Wright, D.P.
1992 'Unclean and Clean (OT)', in *Anchor Bible Dictionary*, VI (New York: Doubleday): 729–41.

Yadin, Y.
1983 *The Temple Scroll*, I-III (Jerusalem: The Exploration Society).

Zeitlin, S.
1973 *Studies in the Early History of Judaism* (New York: Ktav).

Zevin, S.J. (ed.)
1989 '*Tahorah*', in *Entsiqlopedyah Talmudit*, XIX (Jerusalem: Talmudic Encyclopedia Publishing): 1–71.

Zias, J.
1999 Oral Presentation at Qumran Section, Society of Biblical Literature Annual Meeting, Boston, MA (unpublished).

Indexes

Index of References

Hebrew Bible

QUMRAN

Rabbinic Literature

Index of Authors

Made in the USA
Lexington, KY
27 November 2011